NICARAGUA:
SOME URBAN AND REGIONAL ISSUES IN A SOCIETY IN TRANSITION

<u>**CONTEMPORARY ISSUES IN SOCIAL SCIENCES**</u>

This is series addresses current debates in the Social Sciences.
Short books will be authored by experienced academics with active
research interests in the relevant areas. Collections of papers
reporting up-to-date research on à single issue or theme will also
form part of the series, as well literature reviews and evaluations of
public policy.

<u>Current Titles</u>

Pamela Abbott & Roger Sapsford :   <u>Community Care for Mentally</u>

<u>Handicapped Children</u>

Allan Cochrane :   <u>Developing Local Economic Strategies</u>

Doreen Massey :   <u>Nicaragua</u>

NICARAGUA

DOREEN MASSEY

Open University Press
Milton Keynes   -   Philadelphia

Typing and secretarial support: Carol Oddy
Map and photographs production: John Hunt

Open University Press
Open University Educational Enterprises Limited
12 Cofferidge Close
Stony Stratford
Milton Keynes MK11 1BY, England

and
242 Cherry Street
Philadelphia, PA 19106, USA

First Published 1987

British Library Cataloguing in Publication Data
Massey, Doreen
    Nicaragua : some urban and regional issues in a society in
transition. - (Contemporary issues in social sciences).
1. Nicaragua - Economic conditions - 1979
    I. Title II. Series
330. 97285'053   HC146
ISBN   0-335-15518-9

Library of Congress Cataloging-in-Publication Data
Massey, Doreen B.
    Nicaragua : some urban and regional issues in a society in
transition.
(Contemporary issues in social sciences series)
1. Urbanization - Nicaragua - Managua
2. Rural - urban migration - Nicaragua - Managua
3. Nicaragua - Economic conditions - 1979
4. Rural development - Nicaragua
    I. Title II. Series
HT128. N5M37 1987   307.7'6'09728513   87'22140
ISBN 0-335-15518-9 (pbk)
Printed in Great Britain by J. W. Arrowsmith Ltd,, Bristol.

CONTENTS

CONTENTS

Map 1 : Nicaragua

CHAPTER 1 : INTRODUCTION

Some history

After decades of brutal dominance, the dictatorship of the Somoza
family over Nicaragua finally collapsed on July 19th, 1979. Anastasio
Somoza Debayle had fled two days earlier, to Florida, taking a group of
his closest supporters with him. The Nicaraguan people who marched
into their capital were led by the FSLN,the Frente Sandinista de
Liberacion Nacional. The Sandinistas took their name from Augusto
Cesar Sandino, also a fighter for national liberation, murdered in 1934
on the orders of a previous Somoza. The name Sandino had been banned
from use.

This had already been a long and interrupted struggle, against
poverty, repression and US dominance, on this strategic isthmus which
stretches from the chain of volcanoes down the Pacific coast to the
long slope to the Atlantic on the east. The two sides of the country –
Atlantic and Pacific – are separated not only by the chain of mountains
which runs down its central spine, high, cold and wet, but also by
differences of history and of culture. On the Atlantic side,
colonisation was by the British, in an extension of their slave-trading
interests in the Caribbean. The population is a mixture of indigenous

1

Map 1 : Nicaragua

American indians, and the descendants of slaves. English and indian languages dominate. But this is a small part of the Nicaraguan population. Most people live on the Pacific side, around the large lakes (Lake Nicaragua and Lake Managua), in the mountains to their north, and especially on the coastal plain. This part of the country was colonised by the Spaniards, and it is their influence - in architecture, in language, in links with the rest of Latin America - which dominates today. The total population of the country is about 3 million.

The Spaniards had withdrawn in 1821, as part of a wider settlement in Latin America of the end of their decaying formal empire. Politically, they left behind them a power vacuum in which two groups of families, the Conservatives and the Liberals, battled with each other for control. The Conservatives were 'aristocratic landowners, cattle ranchers and large merchants, descendants of the colonial military and bureaucratic elites, backed by the Church hierarchy' (Black, 1981, p.4), while the Liberals, 'part of a regional wave of Liberalism influenced by English notions of free trade' (p.5), were smaller landowners, and artesans, anxious to cut loose from colonial stagnation and to produce for wider export markets. Each faction had its own city base, the Conservatives in Granada and the Liberals in León, with their own economic links, power structures, and even ports for foreign trade.

The power vacuum also provided an arena for competition between the newer colonial powers, in particular Britain and the USA. In 1823, just two years after the end of the formal Spanish empire, the USA announced the Monroe Doctrine and its interest in Nicaragua was later further heightened by the possibility of building an inter-oceanic canal. The country was thus declared of special strategic interest. In 1853 an individual adventurer from the USA, one William Walker, landed in Nicaragua and after a few victorious battles declared himself president, a position in which he received 'immediate diplomatic recognition from the United States Government' (Black, 1981, p.6). He was overthrown within two years. Meanwhile the English were establishing their commercial interests on the Atlantic Coast. In 1847 they set up the 'Mosquito Kingdom' protectorate and appointed a local king.

But by the end of the 1850s it was a combination of Conservative and US interests which reigned supreme. The Liberals had lost out as a result of their futile support for Walker, and the USA gradually expelled the English interests. For the second half of the nineteenth century, Nicaragua languished under the economically backward and socially repressive rule of the Conservative grandees of Granada.

By the turn of the century this rule was once again under challenge from the ambitions of the agro-exporting bourgeoisie, based in particular in coffee-production. This 'new liberalism' was more modernising and nationalist than the liberals of León. It had its base more in Managua, a mestizo city in contrast to the heavy Spanish dominance of Granada. But the new independence again came into conflict with the policies of the USA, and the Liberal government of Zelaya was overthrown and the Conservatives installed once again. The emerging prominence of Managua was set back for a few more decades (CIERA-UNRISD, 1984, p.8).

The historical backwardness and incompetence of the Conservatives, still content to sit it out in a decaying colonial latifundismo, allowed their backers, the USA, to take even more control of the economy. It was at this time that US direct intervention in Nicaraguan financial interests was established. The civil war also continued and in 1912 a rebellion led by 'El Indio' Benjamin Zeledon, a liberal moderniser, but this time with wide popular support, was brutally put down outside Masaya. In the 20s, Sandino was killed and the resistance by his army, fighting from liberated zones in the mountains of the north, was likewise repressed. The rule of the Somozas, and of the Guardia Nacional, began.

But gradually, from the 20s to the 40s, the importance of agricultural exports, and in particular coffee, was established. In these two decades this one crop accounted for about a half of total Nicaraguan export earnings. The form of this late entry by Nicaragua into the international capitalist economy exacerbated the geographical uneven development within the country. The increasing importance of coffee reinforced the already-established dominance of the western part of the country, and in particular of the Pacific slope. Moreover the problems of such heavy dependence on one crop soon made themselves felt with the steep fall in coffee prices between the late 1920s and late 1930s. Faced, as a result, with declining incomes, the coffee-owners extended their landholdings even further and thousands more peasants were expelled from their smallholdings to join those made landless in the initial expansion of the coffee-growers. They now found work as labourers on the plantations on land they used to work for themselves. Some would be permanent workers, sometimes with a subsistence plot, others could only get seasonal labour, in the picking season. The world depression further worsened the conditions even of those with permanent jobs, as landlords cut wages, turned increasingly to payment in kind, and enforced old semi-feudal relations which kept the workers tied to the land, and to a particular owner (Vilas, 1984; Wheelock, 1975; Black, 1981). One of Sandino's policies which had most antagonised even the relatively liberal coffee-bourgeoisie was the return to the peasants of the land which had been expropriated from them in the expansion of the agro-export economy.

The 1950s saw a diversification of that agro-export model with the expansion of cotton production. And once again the shift in Nicaragua's relation to the international economy brought changes within the country in terms of both social structure and geography. This period saw the development of a dominant financial and commercial stratum increasingly centred on Managua. In comparison, manufacturing remained undeveloped. US policy at the time promoted this pattern of growth, the demand for cotton, and some other raw materials, being particularly strong then because of the Korean war. The US Government's development plan at this time made credit available to Nicaragua for agricultural exports, but not for industrial development (Black, p.37). The financial and commercial stratum which developed, moreover, was itself dominated by a mixture of foreign capital and the Nicaraguan 'grand bourgeoisie' (Vilas, p.114). There were few direct links of ownership between it and production itself.

The expansion of cotton production, though, brought further major changes to the countryside. Once again production was concentrated on the Pacific coast, and once again thousands of peasants were thrown off the land they had been working. In the areas where cotton replaced coffee, tenants and sharecroppers were expelled from haciendas (Deere and Marchetti, 1981). But in most regions it was cereal production that was replaced. It is estimated that, over a decade, 180,000 peasants lost their land and 400,000 acres of the Pacific coast were lost to cereal production (Black, p.37; Carmona, 1984). Cotton soon covered the area between Chinandega and Leon. The ex-peasantry was pushed into the 'subproletariat' of seasonal labour (Deere and Marchetti) or, for at least part of the year, migrated to the cities. In 1955 Nicaragua had to begin importing food.

This double development, of financial and commercial strata on the one hand and of an increased landless population on the other, produced reverberations in the capital city – Managua. The city began to take off again, after the long lull since the overthrow of Zelaya, as the focus of national development (CIERA-UNRISD, 1984, p.8). The financial strata began the expansion of their interests into real estate and urban development. The city centre was modernised and housing built for the associated, expanding, middle class. At the other end of the social spectrum, the newly-landless peasants arriving from the countryside crowded into the popular barrios, and huddled into poverty-stricken settlements along the flood-prone lake-shore to the north (Carmona, 1984). In this period, it was expulsion from the countryside rather than the positive attractions of the city which provoked rural-urban migration to Managua. There was no growth of manufacturing to offer the prospect, however unlikely, of a job there. The only economic attraction of the city to these rural migrants was provided by the expansion of the urban middle class and the consequently increased demand for cheap services and domestic labour.

It was only in the 1960s, in the aftermath of the Cuban revolution in 1959, that manufacturing industry began to receive encouragement in Nicaragua, and indeed more widely in Central America. These were the years of the Alliance for Progress and of the Central American Common Market. As part of the latter, organized to establish a wider market and thereby enable advantage to be taken of economies of scale in production, Nicaragua got the plastic-bag factory. Of the small amount of other manufacturing which was established, most of it was of the 'final touch' or assembly variety, little integrated into the local economy except through consumption, and overwhelmingly located in Managua. Throughout the 60s, the real estate and construction interests continued to flourish in the capital, and the poor from the countryside continued to flood in (Carmona, 1984).

The class structure which emerged in Nicaragua as a result of this chaotic history was, above all, dominated by financial and commercial interests. Internal and external trade, all credit and financing, and

6

all general banking functions, were in the hands of this dominant
stratum, which also controlled most of the processing of agricultural
goods for export. Socially, this stratum was composed of a Nicaraguan
'grand bourgeoisie' which had managed through financial interests to
rise above the rest, by foreign capital most especially from the USA,
and by Somoza. Organizationally, it was divided into three groups: the
Somoza family, the BANIC group (Banco Nicaragüense, with its roots in
the cotton finance of the 50s and with Liberal and US connections) and
the BANAMERICA group (Banco de América, with its roots more in the old
Conservative oligarchy). It was also these same groups which owned the
small amount of manufacturing industry geared to the international
economy. But it was this stratum's control of finance and commerce in
the widest sense, including in particular the financing of all aspects
of production itself, rather than ownership of the direct means of
production, which gave it control over both the organisation of the
national economy internally and its articulation externally with the
world economy and in particular with the dominant imperialist interests
of the USA (Vilas, p.114).

This was also a group which was almost entirely based in Managua,
and with its considerable interests in urban land and development it
had an important influence over the form of development of the city.
Here too the interests of the Somoza family were dominant. Indeed
CIERA-UNRISD (1984) describes Managua in its second period of growth,
in the 50s when it took off again after being set back by US
intervention against the Liberals, as a 'Somocista phenomenon'.

It was, then, what might be called (and what was called)
'unproductive' capital, (i.e. with its dominant interests in the
'unproductive' spheres of the economy, though with links to urban
manufacturing and to agro-processing) which was overwhelmingly dominant
in Nicaragua. And this stratum in turn was dominated, both
quantitatively and in terms of power relations, especially through
control over the state, by Somoza and his closest allies.

This financial and commercial stratum was sharply separated from
agricultural capital. Out in the countryside many of the landowners
had few other commercial interests. Here, as in non-industrial
production generally, with the exception only of mining, foreign
capital was largely absent. So too, with the major exception of
Somoza, was the Nicaraguan grand bourgeoisie. In the words of Vilas

(in translation): 'Imperialism had in Nicaragua more of a politico-military than economic presence, and within the economic their presence was more in the spheres of circulation and realisation than in that of production. Nicaragua never took on the character of an enclave society, so common in the Central American region, and its principal importance for the United States was always its geographical position – the possible site of a new interoceanic canal – and the political faithfulness of its dictatorship' (p.67; see also Wheelock, 1975, ch.VI).

The landowners on whose land were produced the export crops on which the Nicaraguan economy had come to depend were not part of this dominant financial and commercial stratum. But they felt its presence even here in the countryside. It dominated their ability to produce. They needed it for credit, for processing their produce, and they depended on it because it controlled foreign trade. These landowners, Nicaragua's agricultural capital, were themselves highly internally differentiated, varying from very large to a vast number of quite small owners, from those running farms with social relations which were straightforwardly capitalist to those who controlled their workforces through the semi-feudal ties of 'colonato', 'medieria' and 'aparceria', and from those who were energetically productive to those who were frequently absent and much of whose land lay idle.

If the structure of capital and of the ruling class was relatively clear, that of the 'popular classes' was complicated, blurred, and subject to much debate over definition (see, for instance, Deere and Marchetti, 1981; and Vilas, 1984). It is evident that there was little in the way of a classic 'proletariat' in the full sense of the term. The lack of development of manufacturing industry, the importance of irregular and especially of seasonal labour, for instance for harvesting the country's dominant crops (sugar, as well as coffee and cotton, and all of them having their harvests over the same few months), the re-emergence of non-capitalist relations with the price-slump in coffee in the late 20s and their continuance ever since, the vast numbers of own-account workers and artesans and of the permanently 'marginal' in the cities, the latter expelled from the countryside but with no permanent wage in the town – all indicate the smallness of a working class in the pure sense in both country and city in Nicaragua.

On the other hand there was the peasantry, still a substantial class numerically, though vastly reduced in numbers and pushed from region to region by the expansion of the agro-export economy, first coffee, then cotton, and other activities such as the beef-cattle-raising in the southern Pacific coastal plain and in the middle of the country to the east of the lakes. Many of the peasantry were desperately poor, large numbers falling into a group often called 'semi-proletarian' because of their reliance both on tiny plots of lands and on wage labour when available. For the latter, hundreds of thousands of people would travel around the country every year, looking for an income to supplement the meagre produce from their plots.

Most of the people expelled by the expansion of export crops, however, became landless. They formed the bulk of the seasonal workers for the harvest (just to give an example, in 1973 cotton production employed only 23,000 permanent workers, but for the three-month picking season it needed over 200,000: Black, p.69). People who relied solely on this form of income are called 'subproletariat' by Deere and Marchetti (1981), while Vilas (1984) argues in reply that they are a straightforward proletariat which simply cannot find permanent work. In the cities, too, there were tens of thousands of own-account workers, from well-established artesanal groups, to those with regular incomes making tortillas, making and mending clothes, doing washing and ironing, repairing cars and any kind of machinery, to vast ranks of live-in domestic workers, to those who bought and sold, in the markets and in the streets, outside the middle-class restaurants and at every set of traffic lights in the city, whatever they could get hold of.

In economic terms, it is clear that all these different groups, in the town and in the country, performed distinct functions in relation to the overall reproduction of the Nicaraguan economy. But if few of them were easy to classify as 'proletariat' in the sense of having a wage within capitalist social relations, many more of them could be so classified in terms of having been dispossessed of all means of production (Vilas, p.103). Moreover socially the different relations to the wider economy were utterly intermixed. Within each household, even if individuals had particular single sources of income and therefore a particular relation to the economy and formally-defined class structure (which was anyway rare), the other members of the household would certainly have different ones. And politically, the divisions were even more blurred. Not only the dispossessed but also

artesans and small-owners were part of 'the people' ranged against
Somoza, united as Vilas puts it (p.19) not so much by the specifics of
their position within the social relations of production, as by their
political subordination and their poverty.

On December 23rd, 1972, Managua was devasted by an earthquake. Up
to 20,000 people died, over half of the city's housing was destroyed
and 90% of its commercial buildings were damaged beyond repair. The UN
estimated the damage at around $800m (Black, p.59). Somoza's National
Guard set about looting what was left. International aid poured in,
and was used by Somoza and his close circle to line their own pockets.
Tens of new construction companies were formed, many of them controlled
by his associates and he and they cornered the market in everything
from demolition to the supply of building materials (Black, pp.59-60).
Even the streets were re-paved with stones from a Somoza-owned factory.

The form of the city was changed beyond recognition. The centre
was left empty, the roads criss-crossing the open space in an eerie
reminder of the past, and weeds and wild flowers gradually took over
what once had been the central blocks of the capital. There was a
housing boom, in which all three of the big finance groups took part.
Most of it took place on what were then the fringes of the city because
that was where Somoza and his group owned the land. Vast amounts of
money were made in the construction of middle-class suburbs of detached
bungalows. Some of the housing aid was also used to build cheaper
houses. These were put up by the state. What is now called Villa
Venezuela is an example: small houses squashed together in serried
ranks on flat land where it was easy to build. Social segregation was
thereby reinforced (Carmona, 1984). The earthquake hit at a moment
when drought had wrecked food production in the countryside, and
provoked an even greater than usual migration of peasants to the city.
Immediately after the earthquake, there was a mass exit from the city,
but soon people began to return to find a housing shortage even worse
than before. In a telling phrase, Marchetti says of post-earthquake
Managua that it was an anti-democratic city... 'Managua after the
earthquake became the most anti-democratic city that can be imagined —
meaning this in a social sense and even then not exclusively because of
the political regime of Somoza: vast distances, without pavements,
without transport and, obviously, with little in the way of health and

education services. Its only attraction was that life was even worse in the countryside' (CIERA-UNRISD, p.13, translation).

Some themes

This essay is concerned above all with spatial themes in the new Nicaragua. One such theme, though not central to this investigation, is geopolitical: Nicaragua's position on the political map of the world. Since the end of the Spanish empire, and after a brief skirmish with the English, the USA had taken over, and developed the notion of this part of Latin America as its 'backyard'. The 1979 insurrection got rid of Somoza, but there remained two (at least) further issues still to be resolved: what kind of new society would be built and whether or not it would be able finally to establish independence from US domination. The two issues are related. The aggression by the US-promoted 'contra' is a backcloth to everything else that goes on in Nicaragua today. Much of the chapters which follow is concerned with national economic strategy and geographical change within the country. Both have been heavily influenced by the war.

However, the main concern of this essay is not with geopolitics, but with the evolving internal geographical relationships within Nicaragua, and especially with the relation between Managua, the dominant capital city, and the rest of the country. From the brief history just given it must be clear that, as in every country, successive phases in the development of the Nicaraguan economy and society have resulted in major changes in its internal geography. It is clear too that there is a relationship between the development of the class structure, the place of the economy in the international division of labour, and the shifting structure of the country's internal geography, and that that relationship has changed over time. One of the themes of what follows is how this relationship has evolved in the early years of the 'period of transition' since the 'triumph' of 1979.

The central focus is on the relationship between Managua and the rest of Nicaragua. It has often been argued that the concentration of control over the Nicaraguan economy in Managua has been both particularly acute and detrimental to the development of that economy.

The major study 'Managua is Nicaragua', produced for CIERA, the research institute of the Ministry of Agriculture, puts the case strongly, arguing that the overall low population density combined with the high degree of urbanisation 'has been a negative factor in the country's economic development which has limited both the full utilisation of its natural resources and the development of an internal market' (CIERA-UNRISD, 1984, p.12; all quotations are translations), and 'Managua is Nicaragua in the sense that it is the product of a long Somocista history with a particular agrarian capitalist development, of which it is the shop window, and that in great measure it is a shackle which prevents the social and economic transformations which are necessary for national economic development' (p.1). The influx of people to Managua was provoked, as was seen earlier, not by the economic expansion of the city, but by expulsion from the countryside. Thus the engine of the process was the modernisation of agriculture which depopulated the countryside through a form of capitalist development based on plantation agriculture and the import of modern inputs (p.12). Such a process has, of course, been typical of many Third World countries, and certainly other countries of Central America. But the study goes on to argue that the Nicaraguan case, as every case, has a specific form. Firstly, Nicaragua has suffered these processes to a particularly acute degree (p.12). Secondly, and as part of the explanation of this, the processes have a different social basis. 'Nicaragua is the clearest case where the expansion of these activities (finance, commerce and agroindustry) was so concentrated in the hands of one family and its supporters... In contrast to Guatemala and El Salvador where the big producers controlled their own agro-industrial apparatus and gained control of their own financing... in Nicaragua there was a split in the business class across which productive capital confronted those who controlled the activities which were not directly productive' (pp.17-18). Furthermore, and in spite of the far greater amount of land available than in Guatemala or El Salvador, the extent of expulsion of the peasantry from land had been far greater, and the remaining independent food-producing peasantry proportionally smaller, in Nicaragua. (The reason offered for this apparent paradox is that the availability of land precisely led to a greater need by landlords to control their workers, by preventing them having land of their own, a process which led both to a greater degree of underutilisation of land and to a greater degree of rural proletarianisation, certainly in Vilas' sense of dispossession. Finally, even in comparison with Costa Rica: 'The Somozas who amassed such control over the agroindustrial, financial and commercial structure used the state apparatus to discriminate against the agrarian petty bourgeoisie/smaller landowner and to leave them more impoverished than their counterparts in Costa Rica, while at the same time this control over the majority of medium producers and over the peasantry had the effect of inflating the urban population of Managua even more than that of San José' (in Costa Rica) (p.23).

This issue of the size and dominance of Managua is still a major preoccupation in Nicaragua today. And it is some themes around that question which are going to be investigated here. As we shall see, Managua continues to grow in population faster than the country as a whole, and it is that which is the principal worry today. There are two reasons for this: first, within Managua, the difficulties it causes in simply planning for and providing for such an increase in the city's population; second, in the relation between urban and rural, the fear that what the growth of the city represents is a further draining-away of 'real producers', especially the food-producing peasantry, from the countryside and a drift into the (assumed unproductive) life of the city. As will be seen in the chapters that follow, this concern has got very much more serious in recent years as a result of the new economic strategy which the Sandinista government has been pushed into adopting, largely because of the war.

It is easy to see why arguments such as those in CIERA-UNRISD (1984) are worrying. But when they are examined more closely it becomes clear that in fact there are a number of different threads. The first concerns the structure of social relations between Managua and the countryside. What is at issue is the structuring together of particular social relations in a particular spatial form. It is not just the concentration of control in Managua (as though a place could have control) but the fact that that control lay, before 1979, with a financial and commercial fraction of capital which was not only physically separated from the bulk of production, which was in the countryside, but also socially and organisationally separate from it and dominant over it. It controlled production, and the countryside, and it drained it, held it back. It was unproductive capital bleeding

13

productive capital, or so it was caricatured. This is one important element in a longer-lasting characterisation of the Managua-Nicaragua relation. It was in fact not just the geography of social relations (for instance the physical location of control) which was at issue but also the nature of those social relations themselves. What, then, is the situation in the new Nicaragua? How have social relations changed, in their nature and in their geography, in the 'society in transition'?

The second thread concerns simple physical size: the shortage of producers in the countryside while the city continues to grow. This element of the argument is clearly still of major importance. It raises, however, a number of questions: why does the city continue to grow if many of the old mechanisms have been restrained or ended? how, anyway, can one distinguish 'productive' from 'non-productive'?

Within this context of the continuing explosive physical growth of Managua, one element stands out — the continuous mushrooming of 'spontaneous settlements', areas of self-built housing on land simply seized for use by the new residents. These new settlements are the most visible sign of 'the problem' of Managua, both internally and in relation to the rest of the country, and they have become a major political issue. They are likewise an important thread in the chapters which follow. The information and arguments about them are based on a research project, in which I participated, carried out by the Department of Urban Research (DIU) at Nicaragua's Institute of Economic and Social Research (INIES). The aim of the project is to analyse the new spontaneous settlements, those which have been established in the last few years and continue to be established now, in the context of the wider social and economic changes currently underway in Nicaragua. The project continues, as does 'the problem' so this essay is of the nature of a report on the current state of play. I should particularly like to thank Marielos de los Angeles Carazo and Ixy Jaime Martínez, with whom I work as a member of the INIES team. Thanks also to Trevor Evans for many long discussions, and for reading the whole draft.

What follows, then, is an exploration of a particular theme — that which weaves together issues of national economic strategy, issues of class structure, and questions of spatial organisation. And even within this it is quite specific in its concerns. It does not deal with the highly important geographical issue of the Pacific Region; nor does it look in any detail at manufacturing industry, for instance.

14

Moreover, the issues discussed here are not new; they have been the subject of debate in other Third World countries, particularly those trying to develop a more independent and socialist way forward. But because Nicaragua is perhaps less well-known it seemed useful to document its experience. For the same reason, it seemed necessary to provide some general introduction to Nicaragua, as a context for the discussion of the more specific topic. That is the function of this chapter and the next.

Two final points. First, all the translations from books, articles and documents in Spanish have been done by me. Second, also a question of language, the Nicaraguans refer to July 19 1979 as 'el triunfo', the triumph. This sounds overly emotional in English so on the whole I have not used it. Instead I have used 'insurrection' or 'revolution'. Neither of them, however, carries quite the same meaning nor is quite correct. 'El triunfo' refers to the moment in which one preliminary task was accomplished. 'The revolution' is a much longer process, only now being begun in what the Nicaraguans call their 'society in transition'.

CHAPTER 2 : TRIUMPH AND DISASTER

The insurrection

The overthrow of Somoza was supported by almost everyone in Nicaragua except his closest allies. It was an insurrection backed by a very broad alliance. Many of the ruling class strata, however, had only reached that position very late. Sections of them had long been disenchanted by the 'disloyal' competition of the Somoza family and/or had a more humane concern at the poverty and repression through which the country was ruled. But in many ways they were dependent on Somoza, for he controlled the purse-strings of the state. In 1967 they called a demonstration, and 60,000 people showed up. Somoza surrounded them with tanks, the National Guard opened up with their machine guns, and hundreds of people were killed. It was the end of any serious idea of peaceful change.

The earthquake broke up the bourgeois alliance even more definitively. The profiteering of the Somozas, particularly in the conditions of generalised international economic downturn which soon followed, brought out the discontent more explicitly. But it was a divided bourgeois opposition, economically and politically, and, especially coming so late on to the scene (indeed in many cases only supporting insurrection when it was already clear that it was going to happen anyway), that it was in no position to give leadership. In many cases anyway they didn't want much change - just the same basic system, but without Somoza.

The capitalist class in Nicaragua after the insurrection was therefore in some disarray. Quite a lot of it had left, mainly for Miami, and was busily trying to extricate its assets. Other elements, even though they remained within the country, were running down their businesses and channelling funds abroad. Indeed one of the main roles of local unions in farms and factories in the early years after 1979 was to watch out for this 'decapitalisation' - if proven (that is, if means of production were not being maintained and used productively) it could result in nationalisation. There were other elements of capital which decided to stay and carry on producing, but without much enthusiasm. And finally there were those - called 'the patriotic bourgeoisie', and they were a considerable element - who decided to throw in their lot with the forces of social change.

Resistance and struggle on the part of the popular classes had been a much longer and deeper affair. There had been indian uprisings against foreign takeover, first by the Spanish then by the USA, from the seventeenth to the nineteenth century. All over the country there were in the nineteenth century occasional guerilla battles and sporadic uprisings against both foreign occupation and the theft of land from peasants by larger landowners. There were uprisings and strikes by miners and by agricultural workers against the USA-backed repressive Conservative rule. In 1973, just after the earthquake, the pace was quickening: there were land-seizures in the countryside in the north, there was a big construction workers' strike - the construction workers having gained new power in the post-earthquake building boom, and the sugar workers, both factory workers and cane-cutters, went on strike at the huge sugar mill in Chinandega.

The FSLN had been founded in 1961 and had spent a decade and a half in guerilla work and warfare among the peasantry in the countryside in the mountains of the north. What were later to be the agricultural workers' and peasants' unions (ATC and UNAG) grew out of their work here, among permanent agricultural workers, temporary landless labourers, and peasant smallholders (Deere and Marchetti, 1981). But by the second half of the 70s, when the FSLN had clearly taken the lead in organising and expressing the national discontent, the battle had shifted to the towns. And this is important for the story here.

There were early abortive urban confrontations, some later judged to have been errors, others in which popular discontent simply overtook whatever strategy the Frente had had (Weber, 1981; Black, 1981). Somoza took vicious revenge each time... in Masaya three times, in Estelí twice, Ocotal was one of the first towns to be bombed, Chinandega was, it seemed to the inhabitants, 'totally destroyed' (Black, p.131)... León, Estelí, Masaya and Chinandega came to be known as the four 'Guernicas' of Nicaragua. Managua was late on to this scene, but simply because it was the capital it was crucial. The base of the insurrection was in the solid 'barrios orientales' (the eastern quarters), which were, like a number of the other towns, under popular control. Somoza ceaselessly bombed the capital city as his control over the country disintegrated.

In all of these urban battles the 'barrio' (a district, or area, of a town) was central. It was the barrio which was the organisational base of most of the discontent and of the popular resistance. There were a number of reasons for this. Firstly this was not a struggle with the urban/industrial proletariat, strictly defined and organised around workplaces, at its centre. This was one element in the Frente action and had been the centrepiece of the strategy of one tendency (the Proletarian Tendency of the FSLN). But, as has already been seen, due to the nature of economic development thus far in Nicaragua, the working class in a formal sense was very small. It was also fragmented and had tended in its claims to be highly economistic (see, for instance, Vilas, 1984). The bulk of the urban population was not organized into major workplaces. Where they worked in manufacturing it was more usually in small workplaces and most people worked in what is in Nicaragua, and elsewhere, referred to as the 'informal sector' (of which, more later). This urban employment and social structure was particularly marked in Managua. Moreover, some of the biggest individual concentrations of a classic industrial proletariat were in isolated locations, for instance far away to the north in Chinandega.

None of this means that 'working class' people in the formal sense did not play an active role in the insurrection. Indeed Vilas (1984, pp.169-77) produces evidence to show that they played more than a

19

'proportional' role. Weber (1981) on the other hand, stresses the dominant importance of what he calls the 'urban marginals'. There is no doubt that in numerical terms it was the latter group (defined as the urban poor outside of the formal relations of medium and large capitalist production) which formed the bulk of those who did the fighting, and of those who died. But artesans and small owners also threw in their weight. The more important point for the discussion here is not 'who' did the fighting (though it is relevant) but on what social basis they were organised. And this was the barrio. Given this, and given also the point made in chapter 1 that formal sector workers, informal sector workers and artesans, the whole spectrum of the urban popular classes, are intricately intermixed in household structures and residential areas, it is unsurprising that a whole spectrum of groups was involved.

In some cases a particular form of social coherence of a barrio seems to have been an important element in its militancy. The classic cases are the indian barrios of Monimbo in Masaya and Subtiava in León. Monimbo was the first to rise, a trigger for the final insurrectionary storm. Its base, like that of much of Masaya as a city, is in artesanal production. Armchairs are the best-known local product, but there are also all kinds of other wooden goods, and pottery. There is a huge market in the town, and Masaya craftwork is brought into Managua today to be sold. The organisational base of production in Monimbo is the family, relying on hand and craft skills, often making themselves what machinery they need. The claim is of a link back to indigenous indian crafts. It is a classic artesanal structure, and one of the few places in Nicaragua along the Pacific coast where there is a noticeably indigenous indian tone to the social and physical fabric. It was Monimbo that first blew up; something exploded into an uprising. Today, the folk-memory of that moment links artesanal skills to the barrio's militancy in treasured descriptions of the intricately hand-made bombs...

More generally, barrios had been an important base for organisation since well before the insurrection. In many of the towns, but particularly in Managua, the barrios themselves had been initially established through the collective action of illegal land-seizures, though in those days of Somoza they frequently met with a violent response and military repression. Civil Defence Committees (CDCs) had

20

also been formed around basic economic and social demands, and these were to be the forerunners of the post-79 Sandinista Defence Committees (CDSs).

In Managua the importance of the barrio as an organisational base was reinforced by the spatial structure of the city, and especially by the inheritance of the earthquake of 1972 and Somoza's response to it. Barrios were clearly defined and demarcated, groups of them separated from others by stretches of empty wasteland. Above all, there was no centre to the city, no place to march to, to converge on, to demonstrate discontent. The Palacio Nacional, object of dramatic takeover in 1978, was there of course, but not much else. This spatial structure of the city was important also in the development of military tactics; the deep flood-channels which carve their way between the barrios provided good defensive ditches; the open spaces made look-out easier, at least to attacks by land; the paving slabs with which Somoza had lined the streets from his monopoly-producer factory were prized up and used against him.

The political content of the barrio-level organisation in the years before the insurrection is hard to generalise about. The CDCs, for instance, varied enormously. In Estelí and Masaya, for long militant cities, they were powerful and well-organised, and in Estelí in their successor form as CDSs remain so today. They also seemed (and seem) in Estelí and some other towns to have an overtly political content. This was not generally the case. An INIES study of CDSs today in Managua included an assessment of their historical base in pre-1979 CDCs. The conclusions of the study stress the dominance of material demands, and also the often sporadic nature of the organisations. It was not often that their immediate economic and social demands led to wider issues or to deeper political claims.

All of this, the significance of the towns and especially of Managua in the final overthrow of Somoza, the centrality of the barrio as the level and focus of organisation, and the nature of that organisation (the kinds of claims made) is important in understanding what is happening in Managua today.

The physical inheritance

The physical and social landscape which the new society inherited in 1979 reflected all this history. The period of formal colonialism was clearly still present in the division between the Spanish Pacific coast and the British-influenced Atlantic, in the culture of each, in the cultural non-understanding between them, and in the political problems which this posed. Major regions of the country, particularly on the Pacific side, were dominated by the social relations and physical forms of one or other of the few bases of Nicaragua's agro-export position within the international division of labour. Coffee, which had been the earliest of these, was now grown mainly in the hills to the north of Matagalpa. South of the town are the 'beneficios' where the beans are prepared and bagged for export. There is a secondary centre of production in the 'coffee hills' not far from Managua, behind Granada and Masaya. In the producing areas the slopes are covered with the low bushes and it is to these slopes that the tens of thousands of seasonal pickers come each year in the effort to get out the country's major dollar-earner. Today the harvest is an important meeting-time between urban and rural Nicaraguans; in 1985-6 whole Managua ministries shut down for the height of the harvest and everyone went picking coffee. At these times the area south of Matagalpa, where the beneficios are, is full of piles of beans and bags.

Around León, at the same time of year, the fields of cotton bushes turn white and along all the little roads bump lorries which are more than anything like wire crates on wheels, taking the cotton balls to the gins which form this area's agro-processing industry, and which clean the cotton and prepare it, once again, for export. Further north still, around Chinandega, the harvest is even more hectic, for here the crop is sugar. Vast expanses (for Nicaragua) of the tall grey-green waving fields, and the ceaseless shuttle of lorries carrying cane to the mills, which loom like great castles in the fields. The lorries rush as fast as possible because cane soon loses its sugar content. To the south on the Pacific side, down towards Costa Rica, and also further to the east between and beyond the lakes, the pace seems slower. These are the areas of cattle-ranching for the export of beef (once - before the blockade - for the USA, for hamburgers, because this is considered low-grade meat, being fed on grass rather than corn). Regions dedicated to and dominated by the need to export, but in the

22

immediate aftermath of the war and the insurrection, seriously underproducing; in part because of the long history of landlords leaving land idle, in part as a result of the war, in part because of owners leaving the country and destroying what they could not take with them. A large proportion of the cattle herd had disappeared over the border, coffee production was seriously reduced (blamed on a plant disease the effects of which the union disputed), factories were idle and some had been destroyed.

The scattering of medium-sized towns equally reflected both long-term and more immediate history. Granada with its heavy Spanish grandeur of squares, churches and colonnades; León with its university. But all of them still bearing the physical marks of the war. In Masaya, empty shells of buildings line one side of the main square, and the big market, once an elegant stone building its style redolent of Spanish colonialism, lies derelict, empty and overgrown with weeds. The whole town is covered with political graffiti, the silhouette of Sandino and the red and black flash of the Sandinistas, and the slogans and the initials of all the parties and mass organisations. In the middle of it all the battered cathedral still slumbers in the heat. And outside the town on the fortressed-hill where 'El Indio' Benjamin Zeledon fell in 1912 are hung the letters FSLN.

In León : the edge of the market

A street in León

The central square in Ocotal

24

All the towns share the mixture of political graffiti and war damage. In León the walls of many barrios are riddled with bullet-holes, and across the street from each other an old military-post and a small church both lie in ruins, result of a battle between the Frente, fighting from the church, and the National Guard. In Managua too, in the barrio of Nicarao the house-walls still bear the bullet-marks, or else small patches of new plaster where people have found the resources to fill them in; Bello Horizonte was bombed. Since the earthquake, Managua had had no centre, and extensive areas still lay undeveloped; Somoza's ring-roads sliced between spontaneous settlements of one-room wooden houses spaced-out so people could grow some maize and rear a few animals, and many of the factories had been destroyed in the war. It could not have looked less like a city rapidly approaching a population of one million people.

In the central area of Managua

In Managua, looking north towards the lake

Map 2 : Managua

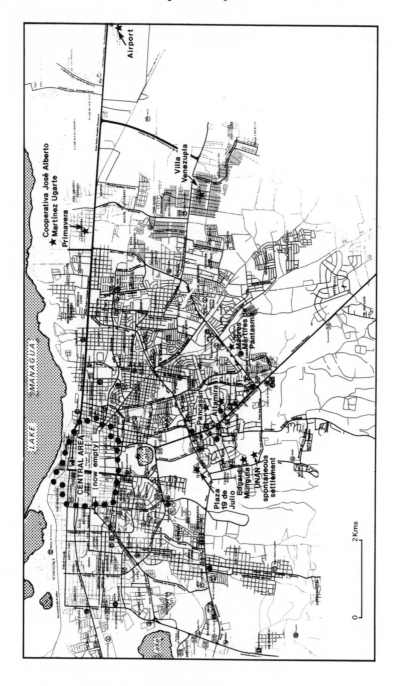

CHAPTER 3 : EARLY ECONOMIC STRATEGY AND SOME INTERREGIONAL IMPLICATIONS

The economic inheritance and the strategy of reconstruction

If the physical landscape which the Sandinistas and the Nicaraguan people inherited from Somoza was desolate and battered by the war, so too was the economy. The effects of the war on production had been devastating. ECLA reported that in 1979 levels of production dropped to those of 1962. UN estimates put the direct damage to the economy at around $480m while at least $1.5m was taken out of the country (CEPAL, 1981). But it was the longer term structure of the economy which posed the most intractable problems. The Nicaraguan economy's position within the international division of labour condemned it to extreme fragility and dependence.

Fundamentally, the Nicaraguan economy was (and is) an agro-export economy of the type classic to the 'old international division of labour'. From an overwhelmingly agricultural base, its exports to the world economy consisted of a small number of primary commodities. In Nicaragua's case by the late 1970s there were four main such commodities, between them accounting for over 60% of export earnings: coffee (31%), cotton (22%), meat (11%) and sugar (3%) all of which were exported virtually unprocessed (Ministerio de Comercio Exterior). The dependence inherent in this position of exporting to the world economy such a narrow range of primary goods was exacerbated by the restricted geographical spread of markets. Dependence on the United States was considerable. Although the significance of the US market had historically been declining (<u>Barricada</u>, Lunes Socioeconómico, 23.5.1983), and although it varied considerably between commodities, in 1978 the United States was still the destination for 23% of all Nicaraguan exports by value. In the same year it was also the source of 31% of all Nicaraguan imports (by value).

The bulk of this agricultural production for export took place on large and medium-sized estates owned and controlled by Nicaraguans. This can be seen from table 3.1.

Table 3.1
DISTRIBUTION OF PRODUCTION OF THE MAJOR EXPORT CROPS, BY SIZE OF LANDHOLDING (% OF PRODUCTION, 1971)

	Cotton	Coffee	Beefcattle[1]	Sugarcane
Large (>500 manzanas)	42	20	19	78
Medium (51–500 manzanas)	52	58	29	18
Small (< 50 manzanas)	6	22	52	4

1 Large : > 1000 manzanas
  Medium : 201 – 1000 manzanas
  Small : < 200 manzanas

Source: Baumeister (1982), cited in Vilas, 1984, p.110.

The degree of foreign penetration here was low. The most important owners were the Somoza family which had nearly 20% of the country's total agricultural production, and a more purely agricultural bourgeoisie. Somoza also controlled large interests in agro-industrial production, and in the financial and commercial channels through which Nicaragua's exports were sold to the world.

It was this 'old international division of labour' model which dominated Nicaragua. The characteristics of the 'new international division of labour' – industrialisation, mainly under the control of foreign multinational capital (whether for import-substitution – i.e. to tap local markets – or for export – i.e. to take advantage of low local production costs) were only weakly developed. The flurry of activity on this front under the aegis of the Central American Common Market and the Alliance for Progress, in the aftermath of the Cuban revolution, never came to much. As elsewhere, moreover, it anyway did little to reduce dependence, though it did do something to alter its form. As was seen in chapter 1, the industries were mostly concerned with only the very final processes in production, and with packaging. Establishing them therefore meant increasing dependence on imports, both of capital equipment and of inputs to the production process, and further increasing problems of external indebtedness. As Harris (1985) points out: 'Although ostensibly designed to substitute locally manufactured products for imported products, this process of limited industrialisation failed to produce an authentic process of import substitution. Nor did it result in any significant development of basic industries such as metallurgy, paper, machine-building, etc. which would have contributed to the integrated industrial development of the economy. It also increased Nicaragua's dependence upon imported goods, raw materials and machinery. For example, one study (Weeks, 1981) indicates that as of 1974, 96% of the inputs used in the manufacture of rubber products, 95% in electrical appliances, 88% in printing and publishing, 85% in metal products and 65% in chemical products were imported' (p.39). The negative effects of this kind of industrialisation on Central American economies were also recognised by the UN's Economic Commission for Latin America (ECLA) (CEPAL, 1982). Moreover, this kind of industrial development was largely controlled by capital based in the United States. US owners held about 80% of the $170m foreign investment in value terms and 76% of foreign-controlled enterprises, comprising 63 US multinationals and 70 subsidiaries (Black, 1981, p.39). Many of the Nicaraguan-owned industries producing for the Central American Common Market, on the other hand, were owned by Somoza.

The Nicaraguan economy's link into the international capitalist economy was largely managed by a number of small but very powerful

31

groups of capital based in finance and commerce. As was seen in chapter 1, this stratum had begun to grow up with the cotton-boom of the fifties and Nicaragua's full insertion into the international capitalist system. By the seventies there had developed groups with major interests in a wide range of sectors, but with particular control over finance and commerce and agro-industry (through which constellation of interests they controlled, though they did not own, agricultural production), manufacturing, construction and real-estate (Wheelock, 1976, chapter VI; Vilas, 1984, p.116).

A fundamental question which the Sandinistas faced on coming to power in 1979 was what to do about this dependent position within the world capitalist economy. It was a position of economic subordination in a number of ways: through import-dependence, dependence on a few primary-commodity exports for which terms of trade were declining dramatically over the long term, increasing international indebtedness (over 20% of exports by the late 1970s), and a particular economic subordination to the United States.

In the short term, it seemed clear that little could be done to change this basic agro-export relation to the international division of labour. It was necessary to earn dollars for unavoidable imports and not possible in the short term to develop other major sources of exports. The four agricultural commodities would have to remain key to the national economy; the main dollar earners. In this context a number of large investment projects were begun, with a view to modernising production and increasing productivity. The huge sugar development at Timal (Tipitapa-Malacatoya) is the biggest such agro-industrial investment. It is primarily geared to improving sugar production because sugar is an important export, but it is hoped also to produce energy from sugar bagazo. The basic finance comes from Cuba (around $90m US), but the Nicaraguans have had to contribute almost as much to the overall budget. It represents therefore a huge commitment to an agro-export model of this type.

But while having decided to accept the basic outlines of that model, the Sandinistas were also determined to alter its balance and the wider social implications of the way in which it functioned. It was called the Strategy of Reconstruction.

First, consumption of basic foodstuffs and other goods by the population at large had to be increased. This was one of the basic

32

aims of the revolution. It implied increased production within Nicaragua of, for instance, basic grains (maize and beans). Irrigation projects were begun for the cultivation of maize in the Pacific coastal region, for instance. It also in some ways implied increased pressure on foreign trade. This was partly because it involved increased imports of foodstuffs. Nicaragua had begun importing basic foodstuffs in 1955 with its full insertion into the international economy as an exporter of primary commodities, with the expansion of cotton production and the resultant expulsion of many grain producers from their land (see chapter 1). The increased pressure on foreign trade was also partly because in some cases (e.g. cooking oil) goods were retained for local consumption rather than being exported. Prices of basic foods were controlled and heavily subsidised, and systems for the distribution of basic goods established (from state purchase from the producers to state or popularly-selected retail outlets).

Second, there was a programme of Agrarian Reform, and major changes were introduced in the property relations of production. Land titles of people who had been working land without formal ownership were fully recognised. In the first stage of the Agrarian Reform all Somoza's land, together with that of his close associates, was confiscated. In total, this amounted to about two million acres of land and 20% of the country's agricultural production. Such land consisted mainly of extensive holdings devoted to the production of export crops, and on confiscation most of it was organised into large state farms. Arguments about economies of scale in production, together with the commitment to export crops, and a commitment to an agricultural proletariat, were the basis for continuing with large estates employing large numbers of workers. But social conditions were changed dramatically. Semi-feudal relations of production were abolished (Vilas, 1984, pp.116-17), wages were increased, social facilities were provided as part of the unit of production, and the farmworkers' union (Asociación de Trabajadores del Campo – ATC) became a significant political force. This first stage in the Agrarian Reform still left a considerable rural-agricultural capitalist class. But here too there was an attempt to escape from the dynamic of individual capitalist production. In relation to labour, wages were controlled, while employment legislation and the power of the ATC ensure some social control over the labour process and daily conditions of production. On the financial and commercial side, many of the functions of the previously all-powerful holding groups have been taken over by the state. Banks have been nationalised, all major import and export trade is handled through the state at administered exchange-rates and finance for investment is provided through state credit. In effect the agricultural capitalist class is simply required to administer the unit of production, and is guaranteed a modest profit for doing so - the Sandinistas say they are converting this class from being capitalists into being 'an administrative bourgeoisie'.

The second stage of the Agrarian Reform ate still further into the rights associated with large private landownership, and further reinforced the idea that the ownership of the means/conditions of production had to be associated with effective production. This stage was confined to estates of over 500 manzanas in the Pacific region and over 1000 manzanas elsewhere (in Central America, a manzana is about 1.75 acres). In this second stage, land was bought up where it was deemed to be unproductively used. Such landownership is a huge problem in Latin America generally where land is frequently held as a basis of social and political power rather than as a basis of production; much of it is therefore left to lie unused. In the case of Nicaragua there was a clear distinction between this kind of landownership, largely in the hands of the traditional big agricultural bourgeoisie, and that of medium-sized landowners. The concentration of land in the hands of the former group was far greater than that of agricultural production (Vilas, 1984, p.117), clearly indicating the low levels of productive use of their land. Much land was held idle, other areas were rented out. Vilas reports that only about 35% of the big landowners lived on their land; half of the others only went there for the harvest and the rest hardly showed up at all. This behaviour can in part be explained as one aspect of the more general 'non-capitalist' character of this class. It also resulted from the fact that these landowners would often not have enough capital fully to develop their land for productive uses. They would therefore be faced with the choice, either of continuing with these 'unentrepreneurial' forms of behaviour or of obtaining credit for development, but only on condition that they submitted to the effective control of the newer, and indisputably capitalist, financial and commercial groups (Vilas, pp 116-7). In contrast to the large landlords, the medium landowners had little

34

choice. Their relation to the land was primarily productive; land was the basis for agricultural production for profit. Vilas classifies this as an 'economic property relation', but one which placed this group of landowners very much at the mercy of big financial and commercial capital. In this second stage of the Sandinista Agrarian Reform it was above all the under-used landholdings of the first group which were vulnerable to take-over, in other words those of the less capitalist elements.

This stage of the Agrarian Reform also affected major landowners who leased land. This was one element in a wider attempt to eliminate large rentier landlords from the countryside (Baumeister, 1985, p.26), a strategy which also involved major reductions in ground rent and the elimination of the remaining forms of sharecropping. And all these measures, as Baumeister points out, reflect the pre-revolutionary antagonistic Nicaraguan division between 'productive' and 'non-productive' elements of capital (referred to in chapter 1), and the post-revolutionary Sandinista attempt to eliminate the latter and to pressure the former into a position of genuinely managing production.

In this second stage, the most important political emphasis was on organising the land into cooperatives (either of a credit-and-service kind or fully-integrated production cooperatives). It was at this stage that the peasants' union (UNAG) was formed. Peasant smallholders until this point had organised as part of the agricultural workers' union, the ATC. Their establishment of a separate mass organisation at this point was a clear recognition of the different concerns of the two groups. As a rough rule-of-thumb individual peasants and cooperatives were more concentrated in the production of basic foodstuffs (see table 3.2) than in export crops. The attempt, then, was to increase food production, and to maintain the production of agricultural exports while at the same time beginning to change the social basis of that production.

Third, while the overall agro-export model was retained, attempts were made to reduce the dependence it implied. In particular, the geographical spread of markets was expanded, especially to reduce dependence on the US. The strategy was to attempt to broaden the market for export goods to achieve more of a balance between the United

States, Europe, the Soviet block and the Third World, especially Latin America.

Table 3.2
SIGNIFICANCE OF THE DIFFERENT SOCIO-ECONOMIC SECTORS IN 1982
(% OF TOTAL VALUE OF PRODUCTION)

	APP*	Large Private	Medium Private	Small Private	TOTAL
Export agriculture	24	37.3	21.7	17	100
Agriculture for internal market	15.7	14.7	8.1	61.5	100
Cattle	24.7	11.0	30.4	33.9	100
Agro-industry	28	63.9	5.7	2.4	100
Fishing	71.9	–	–	28.1	100
Manufacturing industry	31.3	32.5	22	14.2	100
Mines, energy + water	100	–	–	–	100
TOTAL (OF PRODUCTIVE SECTORS)	37	25	18	20	100

* Area of People's Property

Source: MIDINRA, Ministerio de Industria, and MIPLAN. Compiled in Barricada, Lunes Socioeconómico, 28.11.1983.

Fourthly, an attempt was made to invest in industrialisation. But this was to be a different form of industrialisation from that under the Alliance for Progress and the Central American Common Market. This time it was to be based on processing the country's own resources, and on supplying local needs through the production of basic goods for internal popular consumption. Thus Harris (1985) argues that since

1979 there appears to have been a significant increase in the number of small industries producing products for the domestic market (p.62). And private basic consumption (food, clothing, basic services) rose from 38% of GDP in 1977 to 43% in 1982 (Harris, p.51). In part this was an attempt to escape being an exporter only of primary commodities and to move towards exporting those goods in a processed form. It was also an attempt to articulate more closely the industrial and agricultural sectors of the economy, which had previously borne little relation to each other (Black, 1981, p.210; Barricada, Lunes Socioeconómico, 15.8.1983). There was very considerable investment in agro-industrial projects in the early years. A typical project is that at Sébaco, which is described below. Other industrialisation of a similar type includes projects to move upstream from cotton growing to the production of thread, and a geothermal plant on the Momotombo volcano outside Managua, to make use of local energy resources.

The Momotombo geothermal project. The bottom line on the sign says 'A volcano in the service of the people'.

Sébaco

At Sébaco there is, just now completed, a vast vegetable
canning plant. Set in the wide flat fertile valley,
across which drives the straight line of the Pan-American
highway before climbing the hills to the north to reach
Estelí, it is a huge project. Its production capacity
implies, to feed it, a considerable extension of
cultivation. It is hoped that the output will go both to
the internal Nicaraguan market and to exports.

It is a project which will imply social changes: more
jobs both in growing the vegetables and in the factory
itself, and possibly a reduction in the 'informal'
individualised selling of vegetables which has been so
important in this area. Sébaco is a junction town in the
middle of the valley, where the Matagalpa road leaves the
main highway to go eastwards into the coffee hills.
Always there are crowds of people selling onions, carrots
and other vegetables, and every bus that stops or truck
or car that slows is immediately surrounded by vendors.

Sébaco: the sign describing the project

Sébaco: the 'informal sector' at the road junction

The new factory may also affect the continual, equally 'informal', truck traffic southwards down the Pan-American to the vastly higher prices to be gained in Managua. The Sébaco project is jointly-funded, much of the finance coming from Bulgaria. It is hoped that Bulgaria will also take some of its output.

Implications for 'interregional spatial relations'

The attempt to steer the economy along this kind of path implied changes in the spatial organisation of production, and production relations, within the country. Both the character of social classes and their definition and geographical distribution and interrelation were modified, as were the underlying relations between town and country, and especially between Managua and the rest of Nicaragua. Perhaps most significantly from the point of view of the investigation here, the dominance of Managua in the functioning of the economy was maintained, though it was utterly transformed in its social content.

Look first at that agricultural production which is still in medium and large privately-owned units. Given that the property of Somoza, and land which was not being productively used, was taken over in the first two stages of the Agrarian Reform, many of these remaining private holdings are in the hands of what Vilas calls 'economic property', landowners whose primary relation to the land was always through production. Before the revolution, however, as we have already seen, in reality much power over production lay ultimately with the financial sector in Managua. It was this group which, as we have seen, controlled the Nicaraguan economy and managed its relation with the international capitalist market (Vilas, 1984, p.114). It also had a strong base in agro-industry, particularly in the coffee and meat sectors. The weak link, in terms of integration of ownership, was between production itself, and finance, commerce and agro-industry. It was the latter largely controlled by the grand bourgeoisie which controlled the former. And the geographical base of this group was Managua.

Since the revolution, however, as we have already seen, it has been precisely a number of these functions of the grand bourgeoisie which have been taken over by the state, particularly financial and commercial functions. Thus in terms of the relations and functions of economic ownership, that is control over the overall investment and accumulation process, the state now controls the supply of credit for investment, the supply and price of inputs and the price and export sale of the product. 'Control' from Managua of production in the countryside has thus become more formal, has changed from private sector to public, and changed in its content.

It is not clear that it has simply expanded. Indeed Baumeister (1985) argues that in some ways it has decreased; that the displacement of the previously-dominant strata has produced a process of economic decentralisation which has resulted in the strengthening of the middle sectors in the countryside. Vilas, in his definition of this latter group of private agricultural landowners, and in distinguishing them from the more traditional agricultural bourgeoisie, talks of their 'effective capacity to direct the means of production to determinate uses and to organise and manage the production process - although its subordination to big commercial, financial and agro-industrial capital diminished considerably their real capacity to to manage' (p.118, my

40

italics). The detailed control exercised at almost every stage, from supply of credit to control of prices and marketing, by the old commercial and financial sector is documented by Vilas (1984, pp.119-21) and by Baumeister (1985). What have changed are the social relations of this element of the control 'of the countryside by Managua', and therefore its effects.

One obvious contrast is that in the past the finance sector would be taking a sizeable cut of the profits (where available) in the countryside (see Vilas, 1984, p.121) and thus draining it of productive potential. Today the combination of controls and pricing policies which the state wields, while it may reduce the individual impetus to accumulation, guarantees a positive if modest level of profit. This is precisely the financial implication of creating an 'administrative bourgeoisie'. In recent years this has effectively meant a subsidy to certain regions of production, for instance the cotton regions. This was not intentional (though guaranteeing a positive profit and generating increased production were). The original idea was for the state to take a portion of the profit of remaining large capitalists. Changes in the prices of the commodities, of the inputs and of the cordoba have, however, in the event reversed the direction of the flow.

Other shifts have taken place in the geography and nature of the relations of possession. On a day-to-day level the private owner keeps control over the means of production. More strategically, however, that ownership is now subject to conditions, in particular that the land as the major means of production should be kept within full productive use. Supervision of the maintenance of this condition is exercised both locally, through the trades union and other base organisations in the area, and from the central government in Managua. Finally, while control over labour power in some sense still rests with the large private owner, the balance of relative strengths has been shifted. This has been brought about through legislation and in particular through the local and national influence of the ATC.

If it is possible to summarise, then, it would seem that in the countryside the medium and large landowners which remain, and which operate agricultural production, consist of those elements which in the past were anyway more productive in a capitalist sense. Their freedom of action and degree of effective control was severely hedged about in the past by their subordination to financial and commercial interests

41

in Managua. Today that control has been replaced by that of the Sandinistas.

This group of medium and large landowners remains important. Figure 3.2 gave an indication of the ownership pattern of production in 1983. As can be seen, in spite of the fact that most of the land taken over in these early years was in large estates and devoted to the production of export crops, the largest category of producers of agricultural export crops remains the sector of large private ownership. This sector, however, varies considerably both in its nature and in its significance between crops and therefore, because of the geography of export production, between different regions. In both cotton and coffee, for example, public ownership accounts for a fairly small percentage (13% and 15% respectively, Black, 1981, p.209), but the internal structure of private production in the two cases is very different. Table 3.1 illustrates the situation in 1971. In cotton, although peasant production was important, it was large and medium-sized owners who predominated before the revolution. The larger estates were frequently owned by absentee landlords who let them out to small producers at exhorbitant rents. There was a distinct 'cotton group' of large owners who were 'among the most influential members of the Nicaraguan bourgeoisie, not only through their vigorous role in COSEP (the Higher Council of Private Enterprise) and the agricultural producers' union UPANIC, but as a substantial part of the power base of Robelo's (anti-Sandinista) MDN' (Black, 1981, p.216). It was this social structure of production which dominated the large stretches of cotton country north of Managua, around León and Chinandega. Although large and medium owners remain important, the overall structure has been significantly modified in the years since the revolution. The 1980 expropriation of idle lands was an important measure in the cotton areas. Moreover from the same year large owners of cotton land were required to hire out holdings to the small producers at greatly reduced, and controlled, rents. Rent levels were a mere fraction of what they had been before. (Rents also varied by crop, being higher for cotton than for basic grains - Black, p.268.) These small producers subsequently established their own independent cooperative. In coffee production, by contrast, smaller scale production has always been more important, though there were some large plantations, too, often by 1980 in a sad state of neglect. Coffee production is important above all in the Matagalpa region, with a secondary area of (often even smaller-scale) production around Masaya and Granada. In Matagalpa the large and small producers are now organised separately, with the small coffee growers having split off in 1980 from the Central Cooperative controlled by the big local landowners (Black, 1981, p.271), and established their own cooperative, in part with the aid of the ATC.

On those estates which were once owned by Somoza and his close associates, or which were taken over because they were not being productively used, or were being extensively leased, the change in the geography of the relations of production has been even more marked than on the private landholdings. The state farms are organised into three layers; the 'empresa' or main holding includes a number of 'complejos' which in turn include a number of basic production units, or UPIs. The empresas operate as autonomous entities in terms of day-to-day control, but they are under the ultimate control of the central government in Managua. The fact of control from Managua is of course in many cases again not new. As part of his tentacular economic empire which stretched throughout the country, Somoza's estates would ultimately have been tied in to the central hub in the capital city. The estates taken over because they were not being productively used are however likely to be now more under the control of Managua than previously since the very lack of previous investment kept these big landowners out of the clutches of financial and commercial capital. Certainly they are centres of production and investment in a way they were not before the revolution. Certainly too the social relations of production have changed dramatically. From being highly traditional, even uncapitalist, landholdings often with a workforce held together by semi-feudal relations, they became the basis of the most highly-unionised sections of the agricultural proletariat. They are the power-base of the ATC. Indeed the ending of economic compulsion to work (workers could not be sacked) and the release of the old social ties, produced (among other things) horrendous problems of low productivity on state farms.

Lack of data make other changes in the interregional social geography of production more difficult to surmise, but it seems probable that the degree of peasant production both individually and cooperatively, will have increased. Many more of the peasantry, also, have become owners of their own land giving them legal ownership of the main condition of production. Sale of the product, however, became after the revolution formally controlled through national distribution systems based ultimately in Managua[1]. The transfer of many large estates to state ownership, the ending of semi-feudal relations in many parts of the country, and the large investment projects have all implied an increase in the size of the rural proletariat. Moreover the distinction (in formal definitional terms) between peasantry and proletariat in rural areas may now be clearer. In the Somoza period the position of smallholders was so poor that few were able to survive on their own holdings; most had to seek additional income through some form of waged labour. The improvements won for the peasantry since 1979 mean that this is now no longer necessary.

There were numerous other changes too, which also altered the balance and nature of the relationship between town and country. The system of food subsidies was in spatial terms a subsidy to urban areas, the state distribution system of a range of basic goods must have done something (in combination with a cutback in more private non-essential consumption from 38% of GDP in 1977 to 22% in 1982) (Harris, 1985, p.51) to equalise consumption between different parts of the country, the wholesale early provision of rural credits to the peasantry was an effective transfer of resources to the countryside.

The internal economic geographical structure of a country, as we have already argued, has to be understood in the context of that country's position within the international division of labour. In Nicaragua's case, these early years did not see any fundamental change in that position, but there _was_ a change in the social relations and structure of its functioning. And these latter changes produced shifts in the geography of the social structure and organisation of production in Nicaragua as a whole.

In the countryside, production and 'productive' capital is emphasised as never before. The less entrepreneurial large landowners have been expropriated, and rentier elements severely curtailed. In Managua the financial and commercial interests which once dominated production in the countryside have been nationalised.

It is clear that in these changes Managua still retained a dominant and pivotal role within the social and economic geograp'iy of Nicaragua. But the social relations of its position have changed

44

dramatically. Before the revolution the dominant banking sector, based in Managua, was in the hands of the Nicaraguan private sector and also to some extent of foreign capital. It was these interests which controlled the financial relations between Managua and the rest of Nicaragua, and between Nicaragua and the rest of the world. It was Managua which was the focus of the country's external dependency. These financial links are now equally spatially centralised in Managua, but under the control of the Nicaraguan state. The same applies to marketing and distribution systems for export crops — the ENCAFE organisation which markets coffee, for instance. It is also true, and this is new, of the nationally-organised distribution systems for food and basic goods. Similarly, the social class implications of Managua's focal position have also been transformed. The 'financieros' of the Somoza days have been replaced by the 'funcionarios' and the politics of the Sandinistas. Here we have only been discussing the geographical impact of some of the major post-79 changes in the organisation of agricultural production. But there are other ways too in which the relationship between Managua and the rest of the country has changed. And it is to Managua that we now turn.

Footnote

1   This double shift sometimes had contradictory political results in the early years, with peasants newly-titled to their land claiming that they had always effectively, if not legally, felt like its owners anyway, while in contrast they no longer felt like owners of their own product because they had to sell it to MICOIN-ENABAS (the state distribution system)! The question 'what is ownership?' is a complex matter.

CHAPTER 4 : INSIDE MANAGUA

Urban Reform

Within Managua things were also changing. From the early days after
the triumph a programme of Urban Reform was instituted parallel to
that of Agrarian Reform in the countryside. The programme as a whole
embraced a wide spectrum of laws designed to tackle urban and housing
problems, most of them falling under the responsibility of the housing
ministry (MINVAH). They were directed at urban areas throughout the
country as well as to whole 'sectors' - such as housing. There was a
law on land use, measures to regulate housing, and laws to control the
ownership of empty land in urban areas. In principle, the urban
reform was conceived of, even in these early days, as part of a wider
planning of the national territory (El Plan Nacional de Ordenamiento
Territorial) (Carmona, 1984).

   Nicaragua inherited from Somoza an enormous housing problem. It
has been estimated that in 1979 60% of the barrios in Managua were
without piped water, sewerage or electricity. A MINVAH survey carried
out nationally in 1983 found that in Managua there was an 'absolute'
deficit of 27,000 houses, that 22,000 were in a 'bad state of repair'
and that 43,000 houses were overcrowded single rooms (Carmona, 1984).

In percentage terms this meant 20% of households in the capital without a home (people would usually be lodging with other members of the family, or with friends), about 15% in inadequate housing, and about 30% in one-room huts. Speculation in land and housing had been rife, especially after the earthquake in 1972. It was the unregulated speculative boom of those years which had left Managua with such an open and haphazard urban structure. It was estimated that by the end of the seventies 50% of urbanisable land was being held empty (Carmona, 1984).

One of the overarching aims of policy in this area was to establish 'housing as a social good rather than a commodity subject to speculation, as family property rather than an investment good' (MINVAH, 1983) and beyond that to work out juridical forms which would establish housing as 'a use-value' not subject to property rights of sale and transfer (Carmona, 1984). In that ambitious context one of the most important moves was to try to curb land speculation. Laws were introduced to force the sale of land held empty, and a maximum size of urban landholding was introduced. It was argued that the spatial form of the city of Managua should be consolidated, that further outward growth should be discouraged and that the aim should be for new development to 'fill in' the enormous, empty areas within the urban structure. This, it was argued, would help dampen speculation in land, would make the most efficient use of existing infrastructure and 'enable urban development with the lowest levels of investment possible' - a reflection of the critical shortage of resources.

Housing itself was from the start a major national priority coming third after health and education. Darke et al (1986), reviewing MINVAH's policy documents and other writings, drew out the following list of objectives:

'1 to prioritise housing resources on the basis of need
2 to redress inequalities between regions and between urban and rural areas
3 to expand the role of the state in housing provision both directly and indirectly
4 to promote popular participation in the process of housing provision

5   to reduce technological dependence

6   to change the institutional and financial context within
    which housing is provided'.

Thus, much of the expropriated urban landholding (see above) was taken
into state hands – including the old central area, devastated by the
earthquake, but many titles have also been assigned to individual
households. There has been a substantial change in the structure of
landholding in Managua since 1979, with the owners of small lots now
being far more important as a proportion of the total. In the case of
individual ownership, in line with the wider objective of converting
housing from a commodity to a use-value, there are restrictions
(though in practice apparently frequently ignored) on the rights of
sale and transfer. An attempt was made in a number of ways to tackle
the shortage and bad condition of housing. In the early years a
number of state-provided housing complexes were built (see Darke et
al, 1986). There were special emergency programmes for particular
barrios with major problems (the Edgard Munguía barrio was built to
house people from a squatter settlement on the shores of Lake Managua,
which flooded in 1982). A materials bank was established to provide
resources for self-build housing developments. But perhaps the most

The entrance to the Edgard Munguía barrio

significant policy was that of the establishment of 'progressive urbanisations' (urbanizaciones progresivas). This policy was an attempt to respond to the critical housing shortage and to the problems caused by the currently unplanned and spontaneous nature of much housing development. What it involved was the 'recognition' by the state of settlements established by (illegal) land occupations. The policy developed in the early eighties, and in some cases consisted of the provision of new areas for self-build housing development together with technical assistance with planning and plot lay-out. In other cases it involved the recognition of spontaneous settlements which resulted from illegal land-occupations in the decades before the revolution, and which had managed to survive. Many well-established settlements which originated in land-occupations in the 50s and 60s were thereby retrospectively 'legalised' by the revolutionary government. So too were some of those numerous new settlements established in the years immediately following the revolution. Recognition of a claim for legalisation brought with it above all security of tenure of the land. It also improved the residents' claim to provision of basic services, such as water and electricity, although these still had to be fought for.

While this policy of recognition was a clear response to the pressures imposed on people by the housing shortage in Managua, not all spontaneous settlements or land-occupations were recognised. Non-recognition, however, would be the result not of any legal considerations or considerations of private property, but of physical planning problems. Settlements which were deemed to be in areas unsuitable for housing (for instance because they were liable to flooding or earthquake-damage) were not recognised. Such settlements continue, therefore, to be classified as 'spontaneous' by the Housing Ministry (MINVAH), but this characterisation rests on considerations of location rather than on considerations of how the settlements were established, their previous formal legal status, or their age (INIES, 1986, p.81).

However, one thing which <u>was</u> central to the process of recognition was popular organisation within the spontaneous settlements, and in particular the degree of organisation through the local Sandinista Defence Committees (CDS). There would normally be a number of elements and/or stages to this organisation. The first and most fundamental step was organisation and campaigning to gain recognition as a legal entity. This was basic. Following that, provision of water supplies and legal electricity (as opposed to elicit tapping from nearby cables) was frequently also a response to further organisation and pressure from the local CDS.

This characteristic of communal organisation is an important aspect of spontaneous settlements in Nicaragua. It extends also to the means by which self-build housing is carried out. Generally, this is organised communally through the local committees rather than on an individual basis. The CDS takes charge both of the overall organisation of building and of the spatial organisation of the settlement. (Darke et al, 1986, point especially to this aspect in their consideration of the generalised 'left-critique' of self-build housing, arguing that the nature of the process in Nicaragua is more likely to promote solidarity and organisational ability than the individualism which may be the result in other places where the process is different.) These levels of organisation and popular participation should not be overstressed. There is no doubt that in new settlements in the early 80s the initial fight for legalisation represented the peak of mass involvement. Even during this process enthusiasm often waned, sometimes due simply to the time it could take to win recognition. If this were won the CDS would settle down to the more routine tasks of managing the maintenance and growth of the settlement and with that, in general, the level of popular participation seems to fall off (INIES, 1986, p.85). In a survey of 15 of the largest spontaneous settlements, done in 1986, the INIES team found 11 CDS in which activity was largely confined to the tasks of measuring out lots, collecting funds to organise the installation of services (water, light and basic food supplies), allocating lots to new arrivals and controlling the sale/exchange of houses. The CDS was also in the majority of cases (12) the channel through which government-generated activities were organised. These would include Jornadas de Salud (Health Days), and especially the highly-popular Vaccination Days for children, Jornadas de Limpieza (Cleaning-up Days), Vigilancia Revolucionaria (Revolutionary Watch Duty), mobilisations for particular events and occasions, and activities in memory of events in, and heroes and heroines of, the revolution. In 4 cases the CDS also called special meetings to discuss pressing problems, had established decentralised structures in which there was wider participation, was actively campaigning at higher levels, and was building, or had built, a Communal House for meetings and community activities. Although in many cases limited, such activities therefore represent an important part of the process by which the residents become organised and active elements in the revolutionary changes. And this grass-roots activity was clearly encouraged by the enabling legislation of the government, which responded generously to these demands from one of its main social bases, the urban poor (Envío, 1986, p.34).

There were other initiatives, too, as part of the Urban Reform – there were major organizational changes in planning, for instance, and numerous small schemes often individually backed by international agencies or friendly governments. Although certainly in a haphazard and disorganized way, quite a lot was set in motion under the general rubric of the Reforma Urbana.

Nonetheless, urban problems continued and in some respects intensified, particularly in Managua. For the city continued to grow, both absolutely and in relation to the country as a whole. This was a long-term phenomenon. In 1940 Managua had accounted for only 7.5% of the total population of Nicaragua, but this proportion had risen inexorably decade by decade, to 10.3% in 1950, 15.3% in 1960, 19.6% in 1971 and 28.1% in 1980, the year after the defeat of Somoza (CIERA-UNRISD, 1984, p.10). More significantly, it had continued to rise in the years since then and was estimated to have reached about 33% by 1986. Managua is now a 'million city', and the problems posed by its size and continuing growth are enormous. The public transport system (buses) is grotesquely inadequate and overloaded, more and more buses are simply off the road due to the shortage of spares (a situation resulting from the shortage of hard currency and the lack of indigenous production, exacerbated by the economic boycott by the U.S.). There is also a chronic shortage of water such that every part of the city is without water (on a planned and rotating basis) for two days each week. Besides this, there are frequent 'unplanned' occasions on which the water-supply fails because of technical problems. The irony of this is made particularly sharp by the fact that Managua is on the shores of a huge lake. However, it is a dead lake, the waters of which cannot be used; all the pollution of Managua

52

over decades has been poured out into it. The cost of cleaning it, for which studies have been done, is far beyond the resources of Nicaragua, particularly in its current situation.

And yet, in the midst of the evidently inadequate infrastructure and increasingly difficult living conditions, Managua was visibly continuing to expand. By far the most visible aspect of this was the city's physical expansion through the continued establishment of spontaneous settlements which continued to be claimed and laid out from one day to the next in numerous parts of the city. Indeed, there was a burst of new land occupations after the revolution, which continued in subsequent years and rose to a second notable peak in the election year of 1984 (INIES, 1986, pp.82-83). These 'spontaneous settlements' became the symbol of the problems of Managua and of its continuing growth. Not only did they seem to provide the most obvious evidence that the population of the city was growing, but their very 'spontaneity' (ie the fact that their timing and location was under the control of their future residents) meant that they frequently bore little relation to planning considerations in regard, for instance, to the use and costing of infrastructure. Such visible growth heightened worries about water shortages and the chronic shortage of public transport.

In this context, the new spontaneous settlements became the focus of popular and government concern about the uncontrolled growth of the capital. It is important to underline what were the grounds for this concern. It did not result from a desire to protect the property-rights of the previous owners of the land seized by the new settlers. Although occasionally this was used as an argument, almost an excuse, in individual cases(see the example at the end of this chapter), this line of argument was never pushed to the limit. Nor did it hold much water with the settlers themselves (again see the example at the end of the chapter). Ownership, particularly of land and housing, in the new Nicaragua, is a matter of human rights, politics and negotiation as much as of the production of a piece of paper. In the case of the spontaneous settlements, they were matters of concern not because of their 'illegality' but because of the problems they posed for planning the city and, more importantly as we shall see in a later chapter, because of the need to hold people in the countryside. Thus Martin (1981) in a study of land-occupations in Managua argued that 'the

53

The UNAN spontaneous settlement, named after its location near the university

reason land-seizures are a problem is not because of the need to safeguard the property-rights in urban land of one of the most parasitic sections of the bourgeoisie (the pre-1979 financial and commercial strata - DM), but because of the need to work out the rational use of a resource which one day will be the national heritage' (Martín, 1981, p.1).

The initial interpretation of the problem was that the new spontaneous settlements were primarily a product of migration from the countryside. There were spates of newspaper articles on the impossibility of loading yet more people into the city's creaking infrastructure. Furthermore, it was argued, these new arrivals could not contribute productively, in an economic sense, to society. Those newly-arriving in the city, it was argued, were unable to find employment in the formal sector and therefore resorted to what were called 'informal' activities. These latter were generally characterised as commercial, inflationary, and certainly non-productive. Indeed the emerging popular understanding was of a dichotomy between a productive countryside and an unproductive, parasitic, city, with the new settlements - characterised as the recipients of migrants from the countryside and as the home of the informal sector - seen as an important key element in the deteriorating situation.

The spontaneous settlements
Such a characterisation of the issues has of course been typical of many analyses of the 'shanty towns' and rapid urban growth of Latin America more generally in past decades. More recently, however, the equations it involves have begun to be questioned (see for instance, Connolly, 1985, reporting on Mexico City). Certainly, it proved to be far too simple an analysis in the case of Nicaragua.

First of all, the relationship between the new spontaneous settlements and the growth of Managua through migration is far more complex than indicated by the simple schema outlined above. On the one hand these new settlements are not simply direct products of new migration to the city. Surveys carried out in the settlements in the period 1984-1986 consistently indicated that a large proportion, and often a majority, of the people living in spontaneous settlements were long-term residents of Managua, and had moved to the settlement from other parts of the city. Thus; a survey by CIERA-MIDINRA (1985)[1] of ten settlements found that 80% of the inhabitants had been living in Managua since before July 1979 : that is, even if their presence in Managua was due to migration there at some point, it was not migration which had taken place in the context of, or because of, processes under way in the revolutionary period. Further, a number of surveys were conducted as part of the INIES project (some are still going on); all of them have so far produced similar results. There was a survey of more than 150 households in Dinamarca, a spontaneous settlement (right across the road from the U.S. embassy) which had been established in 1984. This survey showed that 79% of the population had been living in the Department of Managua (which includes the rural area around the city) since before July 1979 and that only 8% had arrived in the most recent years (1985 or 1986). The overwhelming majority of the inhabitants had been living in the city itself since well before the establishment of the settlement. Similar results were found in a small survey done in a very new and short-lived settlement on the outskirts of the city near the university (the settlement was called UNAN), and a survey of almost all the (20-odd) households in the 19th of July settlement, taken actually as a new part of the settlement was being established, found only two households which had recently arrived in the city. About half the families, at least, had been living in Managua since before the triumph.

None of this implies that there is no major process of continued migration to Managua. It seems clear that there is (see next chapter). What it implies is that there is not such a direct causal relationship between migration to the city and the growth of new settlements. The new spontaneous settlements are a product not only directly of migration but also of the problems of the general growth of Managua and of the inherited shortage of housing, now finding a release. The so-called 'natural' rate of population growth is very high in the city. It is estimated that between 1978 and 1980, while the population of Managua grew by 14.4%, the birth-rate increased by 36.6% (Martin, 1981). Moreover new settlements are a reflection not just of population growth but of new household formation and it has been estimated that during the same period (1978–1981) that also increased dramatically (Martín, 1981).

Further evidence is provided by INIES surveys of the reasons which people had for coming to live on a spontaneous settlement. Overwhelmingly these reflected the problems of housing in Managua (the difficulty of renting, the problems of overcrowding and of having to lodge with family or friends, etc.), environmental problems (particularly expressed by people who had been living in lakeside settlements) and, in some cases – particularly new households and especially single women, the desire to have a plot of land for oneself. In a general way, and one which was not-infrequently expressed explicitly, the immediate 'cause' of the new spontaneous settlements arises from the attempt by the inhabitants of Managua simply to improve their living conditions in a context where the expectations and demands of the majority of the population have been heightened by the revolutionary process itself.

But if it is not the case that the new spontaneous settlements are built primarily by new migrants to the city, neither is it true that all migrants to the city live in spontaneous settlements, even after a brief 'stopover' at the home of family or friends. It seems, although there is at yet little direct evidence on this, that many settle for long periods in other, established, barrios. It is thus only indirectly, through the additional pressure thereby imposed on housing-supply in the city, that their arrival contributes to the forces which result in the establishment of new spontaneous settlements. There are, for example, also considerable numbers of middle-class migrants to Managua. A survey of Altamira, a middle-class suburb in the outer areas of Managua, found a substantial proportion of recent migrants (Delft, 1984). Certainly, too, in 1986 it was possible to see numbers of new bungalows being built on empty lots in suburbs such as Altamira and in nearby, and even more comfortable, Pancasán.

The second main strand in the early popular conception of the new spontaneous settlements was that in employment terms they were dominated by work in the 'informal sector'.[2] One concern which lay behind this interpretation was that the element of in-migration which was from the countryside to the city was not only, obviously, a spatial change but also represented an important socio-economic shift

57

and in particular a change in the balance of social classes away from the peasantry towards the 'unproductive' urban-dweller. This concern grew in 1985 and later as the emphasis on the necessity to prioritise food production increased. This will be explored in a later chapter. For the moment the point to note is that once again the new spontaneous settlements became the focus of concern at the drain of the 'productive' countryside towards the parasitic city. Once again, however, it proved to be too simple an interpretation.

In class terms, it has already been argued that the new settlements were not overwhelmingly the product of recent migration from the countryside.   To that extent, therefore, neither is their establishment a simple and direct reflection of a decline of the peasantry.   In any case, it was of course quite wrong to posit a simple correlation between the informal sector and non-productive activity. In Nicaragua as elsewhere the informal sector is defined in terms of a bundle of criteria which include most importantly the nature of the social relations of production, and the size in employment terms of the unit of production.[3] As such it includes numerous activities which are productive in the sense either that they produce useful material goods (tortillas, clothing) or that they are activities without the performance of which the project of the 'society in transition' could not be pursued. Much of the so-called informal sector in other words did not fall into the category which was the real target for concern and criticism, which was essentially speculative commerce.   Table 4.1 illustrates this clearly.   The figures in that table, moreover, relate only to a person's main employment.   But a significant part precisely of the inflationary small-scale buying and selling which was the definitely unproductive element of the 'informal sector' was carried on by people who at the same time held jobs in the formal sector. Conversely, of course, not only is the informal sector not all unproductive but also not all unproductive activities are classified as informal. This is an issue which will be taken up again in the next chapter.

Finally, even given all these reservations about definition, it seems anyway not to be the case that the new spontaneous settlements are overwhelmingly dominated by informal sector activity. There is not yet as much evidence as in the case of migration, but it is indicative. An early indication came from a survey reported in Martin

Table 4.1

COMPONENTS OF INFORMAL SECTOR EMPLOYMENT, 1982

	Nicaragua (%)	Managua (%)
Agriculture, hunting, fishing	8.0	3.4
Mines and quarries	–	–
Manufacturing	19.0	16.2
Electricity, gas, water	–	–
Construction	–	–
Commerce (wholesale and retail)	34.0	36.3
Transport, warehousing, communications	4.6	4.7
Finance, insurance	–	1.1
Communal, public and personal services	32.2	35.7

Source: Encuesta de Hogares, INEC, 1982

(1981) concerned with the tertiary sector, and which found 58% of activity to be in that sector, a proportion no higher than that for the city as a whole. The CIERA-MIDINRA (1985) survey already mentioned found 40% of employment to be salaried work in the formal sector, 32% to be in the informal sector and 13% of people to be unemployed. In their conclusion they wrote that a large proportion of sectors normally defined as informal were in fact developed in the context of formal sector activities, and that the informal sector was not uniquely associated with the spontaneous settlements.

This analysis of spontaneous settlements is at variance with what was for long in Latin America the explanation of their formation and character. This was an explanation akin to the interpretation which was current in Nicaragua. It is a characterisation which, as we have said, is being increasingly questioned in other countries of Latin America. These results for Managua's recent spontaneous settlements are therefore of wider interest. However, there is a difference; most previous analyses in Latin America have necessarily been done in a more purely capitalist context, or one where it is capitalism which is on the ascendancy. Nicaragua, however, would claim to be a society in transition.

From the emerging evidence it seems that some of the immediate causes in those other countries are also found in Nicaragua.   The shortage and inadequacy of housing is one such element, even if the causes lying behind those housing problems are different in Nicaragua from elsewhere.   But there are some elements specific to the new Nicaragua, at least in comparison with the same country in the days of Somoza. First there is the simple fact that a takeover of land is no longer met by the guns of Somocista National Guards. The importance of this factor is evidenced by the sudden increase in the number of takeovers immediately after the insurrection. This factor, too, has its parallels in other Latin American countries, where increases in such action have been a frequent response to greater formal democracy and/or the reduction of repression.   In Nicaragua, however, the process has probably been more marked.   Moreover it has been reinforced by the fact (illustrated in the story of the Pantasma settlement, told below) that the 1979 victory itself heightened immeasurably both people's expectations of life and their definition of what were their rights.   For many people land occupation was a route, through organisation, to a real improvement in their living conditions, and one which was now legitimately (if not in a formal sense 'legally') open to them as a right gained through the revolution. Moreover it is a right which the Sandinistas, however much they, or the government departments, might argue against the spontaneous settlements, would not wish to deny.   The story of the Pantasma settlement illustrates the susceptibility of both police and housing ministry to such arguments. Third, this understanding was further reinforced by the fact that, in the early 1980s the Sandinistas had granted legal recognition to spontaneous settlements, and had given them the status of progressive urbanisation mentioned earlier. With organisation through the CDS the population had been able to win provision of water and electricity. The result of all this was that the revolutionary process itself unleashed a burst of new land occupations and spontaneous settlements as people sought to relieve the enormous pressures on housing in Managua that had accumulated during the years of Somoza.

Madres Mártires de Pantasma: from an interview with a resident.

'This spontaneous settlement grew up after a land occupation in August 1984. To begin with, at the initial occupation, there were about 20 people, then 40 or 50, but as the day passed more and more people arrived. The first 'toma' (occupation) took place at 9 in the morning. But then people kept on arriving. They were just getting off buses, and appearing from everywhere. By the end of the day about 500 people were there demanding a piece of land. Later people took land by night. They were worried they might be moved on by MINVAH. The person who took possession of the first plot came from Las Torres barrio (near the lake). Her house had been flooded and she had nowhere to go.

The settlement grew through different stages and sectors over a period of 5 months.

The occupation of lands was directed by a woman called Virginia who was one of the first people to arrive. She organised the distribution of plots. The idea was to have plots of a standard size (10 x 30 metres because they said that was the size used by MINVAH), but in the end the size of lots varied. Then people would clear and clean the land and build houses using poles, planks, and bits of zinc.

In those early days, in August, the police appeared and told the people that they couldn't stay because this land was private property and they had to respect that. At this the people said to the police that there had been a Revolution which was of the people and that they were the people, and the compas (compañeros: the police) went away and didn't come back anymore.

Later MINVAH appeared and told the people that this land had many fault-lines and that it was not suitable for building houses. They went away, but came back later with the argument that the land was the property of Managua cattle ranchers, to which the settlers paid no attention. So it was that the most difficult moments were overcome and people began to build their houses with more security.

In 1984 the settlement had 265 houses and a census in 1985 showed it had 365 houses and a population of nearly 2,000 people.

Most people come from neighbouring barrios: such as Reparto Schick, la Fugente, Granada, barrio La Luz. There are some who come from other departments: Jinotega, León and Nueva Guinea, but they are few.

Among the main reasons people come are: lack of housing, not being able to find a place to rent, families living in overcrowded conditions, and people who want to live independently such as when there is a marriage or a free union. Another cause is people coming from war zones, though these are few, or who come to Managua to study, and people trying to improve their living conditions.

Madres Mártires de Pantasma : housing along the main road on the edge of the settlement

Footnotes

1   From the point of view of the present study there are reservations about the selection of the sample of settlements in this survey, not all of them being new spontaneous settlements. For that reason the INIES surveys, see below, are more clearly significant for the present argument.

2   There has been much criticism in the wider debate about Third World cities, of this conceptualisation of a part of the economy as 'informal'. The term is retained here because the concept is, as the discussion will show, part of what is at issue in the debate in Nicaragua, and because it is the term used in that debate.

3   The criteria, and the employment called 'informal', have been changed over time in part in response to debate.

Migration to Managua

Yet if it was incorrect to pinpoint the continuing emergence of spontaneous settlements as the direct physical evidence of migration to Managua, it is nonetheless true that there is a strong flow of migration to the city and a very rapid rate of 'natural' growth of the urban population. 'Of all the countries of Central America, Nicaragua is the one with the lowest density of population, and at the same time the most urbanised' (CIERA-UNRISD, 1984, p.12). In proportion to the total national population, Managua is bigger than Mexico City.

From just under 400,000 people in 1975, Managua reached about 560,000 in 1979, over 850,000 in 1985 and is now generally assumed to have a population of nearly a million (figures from INEC). Table 5.1 recapitulates its long-term growth as a proportion of the total population of Nicaragua.

This increasing dominance of Managua has been part of a wider process of urbanisation. Table 5.2 shows that the rate of growth of urban areas with more than 20,000 inhabitants has for decades, and not unusually, been much faster than that of the rest of the country.

Table 5.1

POPULATION: MANAGUA AS A % OF NICARAGUA

1940	1950	1960	1971	1980
7.5%	10.3%	15.3%	19.6%	28.1%

Source: CIERA–UNRISD, 1984, p.10

Table 5.2

URBAN AND RURAL POPULATION GROWTH (% ANNUAL)

	Nicaragua	Rural	Urban Areas < 20,000	Urban Areas > 20,000
1950–63	3.0	2.2	2.4	6.2
1963–71	3.5	2.8	2.7	5.8
1971–80	3.4	3.3	2.0	6.7

Source: CIERA–UNRISD, 1984, Cuadro I

Table 5.3

DEPARTMENT OF MANAGUA: URBAN AND RURAL DISTRIBUTION OF THE POPULATION

Municipality	1971		1980	
	% urban	% rural	% urban	% rural
San Francisco Libre	11	89	24	76
Tipitapa	28	72	57	43
Managua	89	11	93	7
San Rafael del Sur	16	84	37	63
Carlos Fonseca Amador	12	88	21	79
Mateare	40	60	50	50
TOTAL	82	18	85	15

Sources: National Census, 1971; Anuarios Estadísticos, 1980

Finally, as table 5.3 clearly shows, even within the generally-fast-urbanising Department of Managua it is the capital city itself which has been growing the fastest. Predictions of the population of Managua in the year 2000 rise as high as 2.3 million people.

Furthermore, what evidence there is does suggest that part of this growth of the capital city has been, and continues to be, a result of migration. Within the complex network of migratory flows within Nicaragua as a whole, Managua has for decades been the principal pole of attraction. Table 5.4 indicates, indeed, that the annual rate of migration to the city has over the long term been increasing.

Table 5.4
MIGRATION INTO MANAGUA (ANNUAL)

Year	1950	3,067
	1963	5,800
	1971	14,092
	1980	11,882
	1983	29,393

Source: Delft, 1984

Table 5.4 also indicates, though the figures are really only estimates, that migration has continued apace in the period since 1979. Once again, as in the case of spontaneous settlements, most of the analysis of rural-urban migration in Latin America has of necessity been carried out in the context of capitalist societies. Moreover many of the causes of such migration have been seen to lie in specifically 'capitalist' aspects (including the increasing dominance of capitalist forms) within those societies. It is therefore of particular importance in Nicaragua to try to understand the degree to which such causes continue to be significant, and the degree to which on the other hand other different processes are now operating within this 'society in transition' to produce the descriptively-similar phenomenon of rural-urban migration.

In fact no major systematic study of migration since 1979 has been carried out although it is widely recognised to be much needed (shortage of resources hits research as well as everything else). Nonetheless, from the partial evidence which does exist it is possible to suggest some of the broad underlying causes.

Perhaps most obviously, migration to Managua is as we have seen a long-standing process in Nicaragua, and it is not going to stop overnight even if, as it does, the government exhorts people to stay in the countryside (see chapter 6). Most people in Nicaragua, certainly on the Pacific side where most people live, have friends and probably family in the capital. The evidence is that it is with friends and family, and not in a new settlement, that migrants first live on moving to the city. The social networks are well established for moving to Managua.

More fundamentally, some of the changes won as part of the revolutionary process itself, some of its achievements, have also had the effect of stimulating continuing migration. The abolition of semi-feudal relations in the countryside (chapter 3) freed people from long-standing ties to particular landowners. Heightened expectations of what life has to offer combined with a generally increased mobility to encourage people to seek out new opportunities. The Urban Reform programme (chapter 4) increased still further, and in spite of parallel improvements in many rural areas, the attractions of life in the city over that in the countryside. The lack of military repression of land seizures in Managua, the legalisation of 'progressive urbanisations' in the early years, and the expectation that in the end even more would be legalised, also seem to have had their effect. Even though, as was seen in chapter 4, the spontaneous settlements are not primarily a base for new migrants from the countryside, their recognition may have seemed to indicate that the government, in spite of all its policy-statements to the contrary, was in fact prepared to facilitate a further increase in the size of the capital city, or certainly was not prepared to make life hard for those who wanted to set up a place of their own there. If all social processes are in some sense contradictory, this is certainly true of elements of the process of transition in Nicaragua. As was seen in the analysis of spontaneous settlements at the end of chapter 4, so too with rural–urban migration. Some of the clear achievements since 1979 have in turn stimulated further changes which, as we shall see in chapter 6, are increasingly problematical.

The creation of a wider and more democratic government apparatus has also had the effect of focussing Nicaraguan life upon Managua. Some aspects of this were examined in chapter 3. Above all it has increased the concentration of the anyway growing numbers of professional and administrative workers in the capital city. Most 'middle class' migration to Managua, of course, is not itself from rural areas. It is not 'rural–urban' migration. Much more likely it is from another town, a movement up the urban hierarchy. However this concentration of the middle class in turn gives a further dynamic to a wider process of migration to Managua, and which is more likely to be from the countryside. The higher levels of income lead to higher levels of demand for goods, services and domestic workers. They also lead to higher prices for all these things, thereby encouraging producers in the countryside to ship their goods to Managua, often through quite complex commercial systems, rather than selling them locally. The geographical price–differential in other words encourages trade to be kept out of the formal mechanisms of distribution where prices are controlled, to seek higher prices through the 'informal' commercial sector which is thereby focussed on Managua, and further encourages the concentration of commerce, and migration, on that city. The whole process is fuelled by the shortage of supply (see chapter 6); moreover, to the extent that people are tempted by the high returns which can be earned through informal petty commerce to leave food–production in the countryside the process becomes a vicious circle in which the shortage of supply is exacerbated by the further movement of people off the land. A major study of the centrality of Managua in Nicaraguan food–distribution systems (CIERA–UNRISD, 1984) documents a particularly high rate of increase of this urban informal commercial sector in the first two years after the insurrection. It argues that the main causal factors in this period were the concentration of state workers in Managua, the reactivation of the Managuan economy, and the politics of Urban Reform. Under this last heading it points particularly to the increased supply of housing and the legalisation of new settlements. It recognises that most of the inhabitants of the new

69

settlements were people already living in Managua, and goes on to argue that the new availability of such housing was particularly important for formerly live-in domestic workers, who could now build a home of their own. Thus, an increased effective demand for domestic workers in the city combined with a significant improvement in their conditions, further reinforced by the Sandinistas' long-standing commitment to improving domestic workers' (very low) wages, made — so the study argues — the migration of domestic workers an important axis of a wider flow of people to the capital.

The concentration of 'middle strata' in Managua is of course not wholly due to the location there of the central state. Most of the other national institutions of Nicaraguan society tend also to have their apexes in the capital. This is as true of the mass movements — the CDS, AMNLAE (the women's movement), and even the ATC (the agricultural workers) and UNAG (the peasants' movement) as of anything else. Given the paucity of the infrastructure even between major towns and the consequent difficulty of transport and communication (it can regularly take up to half a day to get a telephone call through to Matagalpa, for instance), it is difficult to see how it could be otherwise. But the effect of this concentration of the middle strata (which is documented in more detail later in this chapter) goes beyond the economic impacts just described. It creates the image of a capital city — like other capital cities — where people are richer, life is better, more 'modern' and more 'cultured', where there is a wider range of services, and where the tops of even the flattest hierarchies are to be found.

It has been argued that a number of other policies have further contributed to the continued dominance of Managua. The distribution of extensive easy credit in the early years to a peasantry without the means, and often without the inclination, to expand production is one factor often cited. The policy of holding down the prices of basic foods in order to improve the living standards of the urban poor, which was one contributor to the peasants' disinclination to expand production, increased the gap between official prices and those which could be got through the informal sector, thus further fuelling the growth of that channel of commercial distribution.

Chapter 3 examined the implications for the structure of relations between the countryside and Managua of some aspects of the early

70

economic Strategy of Reconstruction. This section has shown that quite a wide range of policies, including some of the clear achievements of the revolutionary process, have contributed to the continuing numerical dominance of the city over the rest of the country. The implications of all this in terms of the geography of the class structure will be examined in the next section of this chapter.

None of this should be surprising. One or two major cities overwhelmingly dominate in every way the economies and societies of most Latin American countries and indeed most countries of the Third World. What is different about the Nicaraguan type of case is that the terms of that dominance are different, as are (some of) the underlying causes.

One cause, yet to be mentioned, is particularly different; and that is the war. It is in the rural areas, along the northern border with Honduras, to a lesser extent along the frontier to the south with Costa Rica, and down from Honduras along the central mountain chain east of the lakes, that the war is most felt. It has directly contributed to shortages of supply by making agricultural production difficult if not impossible in some areas. It has led to the relocation of one tenth of the population to areas of greater safety, a process which not only disrupts production but has the effect that, once having moved from their homes, people find further moves, to a town or even to Managua, much less of a big step. And finally in some of these areas the contra are simply a constant physical threat, even if actual attacks are only intermittent. The number of people who would cite 'la guerra' as the prime motive for their migration to Managua is probably smaller than is sometimes thought. But as a background, contextual, reason for a wider set of processes which result in the flow of migrants to the capital, it is undoubtedly important.

Questions of social structure

Given, then, that migration to the city continues apace, and given also the socio-spatial changes analysed in chapter 3, what is the geography of social classes in Nicaragua? More precisely, what is Managua's position within the social structure of the country as a whole?

71

The basic data is given in tables 5.5 and 5.6. It is, unfortunately, for 1980 and therefore does not catch much of the effects of changed social processes in the period since the triumph. It is, however, a starting point, and it is possible to deepen it with other more recent but more patchy data and from knowledge of subsequent events.

The first thing which is clear from a comparison of the two tables is that in terms of social structure Managua is not the geographical base of the (private) owners of means of production. As table 5.5 indicates nearly a quarter of Nicaragua's economically-active population own their own means of production. But these strata are found overwhelmingly in the rural sector. Such owners are markedly less important in Managua than they are in the country as a whole. In Nicaragua as a whole, the combined strata of large and medium bourgeoisie, medium peasants and petty-bourgeois owners, make up 23.5% of the economically-active population (table 5.5), while in Managua the corresponding categories though rather differently divided, simply into bourgeoisie and petty-bourgeois owners, can be seen to amount to only 8.6% of the economically-active population (table 5.6). In the rural sector in contrast 39.5% of the economically-active population falls into this general category of 'owner' (propietario).

There are a number of ways in which this initial broad conclusion must immediately be modified. First of all, this is not a characteristic specifically of Managua but a result of the contrast in social structure between non-farming and farming sectors more generally. This can be seen by comparing the percentage of 'owners' in Managua's social structure (8.6%, table 5.6) with the equivalent percentage in the 'non-farming' sector of Nicaragua as a whole[1] (9.6%, table 5.5), though account must be taken in interpreting this figure that Managua itself is the most important component of this non-rural sector. What this 'urban-rural' distinction reflects, of course, is the importance of the peasantry in the countryside. In table 5.5 the peasantry is mostly classified under the headings 'medium peasantry' and 'petty-bourgeois owners'. In the countryside these categories make up 30% of the economically-active population. In non-rural areas both the social composition of these categories is different and they are of much less significance in the social structure. In non-rural areas the medium-peasant group is obviously absent, while the category

72

Table 5.5

THE STRUCTURE OF THE ECONOMICALLY-ACTIVE POPULATION IN NICARAGUA
(%), 1980

	In agricultural sectors	In non-agricultural sectors	EAP[11] TOTAL
Property owners[1]	39.5	9.6	23.5
Large bourgeoisie[2]	0.4	0.1	0.2
Middle bourgeoisie[3]	9.1	0.3	4.4
Middle peasants[4]	13.0	-	6.1
Propertied petty bourgeoisie[5]	17.0	9.2	12.8
Non-property owners[6]	60.5	90.4	76.5
Salaried petty bourgeoisie[7]	1.0	18.0	10.1
Proletariat[8]	6.7	31.4	20.0
Semi-proletariat[9]	35.5	16.3	25.2
Sub-proletariat[10]	17.3	24.7	21.2
Total economically active[11]	100.0	100.0	100.0

Sources: CIERA, MIPLAN, INEC and PREALC. Figures put together by the Pensamiento Propio Collective, INIES, Managua, Nicaragua. This table adapted from Harris, 1985.

1   Those who possess means of production.
2   Latifundio owners and the Large Agrarian Bourgeoisie defined as those with more than 500 manzanas dedicated to internal consumption crops, or with more than 65 manzanas of coffee, or more than 200 manzanas of cotton, or more than 1,000 manzanas of cattle pasture, with an average of 912 head of cattle. In non-agricultural sectors, this refers to owners of large industrial, commercial and service enterprises which employ more than 100 workers.

3   Those who possess between 50 and 500 manzanas of crops for internal consumption, 15 to 65 manzanas of coffee, or 50 to 200 manzanas of cotton, or 200 to 1,000 manzanas dedicated to cattle-ranching, with an average of 311 head of cattle. In non-agricultural sectors, this refers to medium-sized commercial and service enterprises.

4   Those who possess between 10 and 50 manzanas of crops for internal consumption, or 5 to 15 manzanas of coffee, or 5 to 50 manzanas of cotton, or 20 to 200 manzanas dedicated to cattle-ranching, with an average of 72 head of cattle.

5   In agriculture, non-remunerated family workers with agricultural property corresponding to note 4 above. In non-agricultural sectors, this refers to small industry, minor commerce and independent professionals.

6   Those who do not possess means of production.

7   Administrators and technicians in productive, commercial and service sectors, including state technicians with a monthly income above 1,250 cordobas in 1980.

8   Agricultural workers with permanent employment, as well as salaried workers in non-agricultural material production, government, commerce and services.

9   Poor peasants who possess up to 10 manzanas of land dedicated to internal consumption crops, or up to 5 manzanas of coffee, or up to 5 manzanas of cotton, or up to 20 manzanas dedicated to cattle pasture, with an average of 17 head of cattle. In the non-agricultural sectors, this refers to self-employed workers and artesans.

10 In agriculture, landless seasonal labourers and the unemployed. In non-agricultural sectors, this includes domestic workers and the unemployed.

11 The economically active population (EAP) refers to those who are either working or actively seeking employment, usually including those between 15 and 64 years of age.

Table 5.6
THE CLASS STRUCTURE OF MANAGUA, 1980

	Material Production (%)	Central Government (%)	Commerce + Services (%)	TOTAL thousands	%
Bourgeoisie	0.1	-	0.3	1.0	0.4
Petty-bourgeois owners	1.2	-	7.0	24.4	8.2
Salaried petty bourgeoisie	3.9	9.1	6.0	56.5	19.0
Proletariat	11.8	4.3	13.2	87.5	29.3
Artesans and own-account workers [1]	6.9	-	6.8	40.7	13.7
Unemployed, subemployed and domestic workers[2]	-	-	29.4	87.3	29.4
Total (%)	**23.9**	**13.4**	**62.7**	**-**	**100.0**
Total (thousands)	**71.0**	**39.9**	**186.5**	**297.4**	**-**

Source: CIERA-UNRISD, 1984, p.26

1 Own-account workers in commerce refers to small store and bar keepers, and in services such people as plumbers

2 Includes more than 20,000 domestic workers, and 40,000 unemployed. The remainder includes subemployment and 'informal' commerce.

petty-bourgeois owner, which here refers to small industrial and commercial owners and self-employed professionals is of much less significance numerically within the economically-active population (8.2% as compared with 17%). It is interesting to note, however, that even this category is of less significance in Managua (8.2%, table 5.6) than in the non-rural sector as a whole.

It is worth noting too that the same is true for the most marginal category of small-owner, where ownership and wage-earning may often be mixed. In table 5.5 Harris classifies this group as 'semi-proletarian' (and includes it under 'non-owners'). In the rural sector it consists of very poor peasants who own only tiny plots of land, and in the non-rural sector of own-account workers and artesans (which latter category coincides with that for Managua used in table 5.6). The contrast is once again clear. In Nicaragua as a whole this group makes up about a quarter of the total economically-active population (25.2%), in the rural sector it rises to over a third (35.5%), and is indeed the biggest single group, while in the non-rural sector it is of far less importance, accounting for 16.3% of the economically-active population and coming behind all the other non-owner groups (in table 5.5) in order of numerical significance. But in Managua it is even less important again, accounting for only 13.7% of the economically-active population (table 5.6).

But this greater importance of ownership in the countryside, and in the country as a whole, than in Managua, is not only a question of the peasantry, the non-rural petty bourgeoisie and very small, marginal, owners. It is also true of larger, and clearly capitalist, owners of the means of production. The large and medium bourgeoisie, which are precisely defined in the notes to table 5.5, account for 4.6% of the economically-active population of Nicaragua. In the rural sector this rises to 9.5%, though this will certainly have declined with the second stage of the Agrarian Reform. In Managua, the category 'bourgeoisie' in table 5.6 accounts for a mere 0.4%, a figure which is exactly the same as that for the non-rural sector as a whole (0.4%, table 5.5).

In all of this, it must be stressed, we are discussing the numerical distribution of the economically-active population: the simple descriptive geography of the class structure. This is not the same thing as evaluating the importance of these different classes

76

within the economic and social structure of the country (the numerically-tiny bourgeoisie in Managua may be structurally all-powerful, for instance, as we know it was before 1979). For this kind of evaluation it is necessary to put together the present analysis of the geography of class structure with the beginnings of the analysis of the geography of the underlying relations of production presented in chapter 3, and with an appreciation of the wider social and political influence of the different social groups. The analysis in chapter 3 indicated that, in terms of the private sector, the old dominance of Managua within the underlying relations of production has been substantially dismantled. The analysis in the present chapter shows, moreover, that in terms of the numerical geography of social class within Nicaragua, neither owners in general nor the bourgeoisie more specifically is concentrated in Managua. In these terms it is in the countryside that private property in the means of production is most important, and where the owners of the means of production are concentrated.

Which, then, are the social groups which are concentrated in Managua? By far the most concentrated is the salaried petty bourgeoisie. In Nicaragua as a whole this social group accounts for 10.1% of the economically-active population (table 5.5), but in Managua it is almost double that, at 19.0% (table 5.6). Moreover there is here a clearer difference between Managua and the figure for the non-rural sector as a whole (18.0%) given in table 5.5, which implies that this is not simply an urban-rural distinction but more specifically a characteristic of Managua.

The group which comes second in terms of its degree of concentration in Managua is the proletariat. Here the comparable figures are 20%, for the country as a whole, and 29.3% for Managua. The proletariat, however, is less significant as a proportion of the economically active population in Managua than it is as a proportion of the non-rural sector as a whole.

Thirdly, given the definitions in the notes to the tables, it seems legitimate to compare the 'sub-proletariat' of table 5.5 with the 'unemployed, subemployed and domestic workers' of table 5.6. And here again there is a concentration in Managua, although rather less marked, with this group forming 21.2% of the economically-active population of Nicaragua but as much as 29.4% in Managua.

77

The salaried petty bourgeoisie, the formally—employed working class and the sub—proletariat; not only are these groups the most concentrated in Managua, they are also the three largest social groups in the city and together make up 77.7% of its economically—active population. How does the concentration of these groups within Managua relate to the role of the capital city in Nicaraguan society more widely, and to the notion of it as the unproductive, parasitic city?

Most evidently, and confirming the indications in chapter 3, there is the clear importance within Managua of employment in one or other department of the central state. 13.4% of the total workforce of Managua is employed in central government. Further, two thirds of this central government workforce (9.1% out of 13.4%) belongs to the salaried petty bourgeoisie; in other words the 'middle class'. Moreover, and looked at from the opposite perspective, almost half (9.1% out of 19.0%) of Managua's salaried petty bourgeoisie (and remember that this is the social stratum most concentrated in Managua) works in the central government. Nearly 15% of Managua's proletariat also works in the central government (4.3% out of 29.3%).

But far more important than the state in Managua's social structure, on these figures, is the sector 'commerce and services'. As can be seen from table 5.6, a massive 62.7% of the economically—active population of the city works in this sector, though there are the already—mentioned problems of definition. For Nicaragua the equivalent sector accounted for about 45% in 1978 (CIERA—UNRISD, 1984, p.58) and about 50% in 1984 (INETER—MINVAH)(these figures are reproduced in table 6.1). About 45% of Managua's proletariat (13.2% out of 29.3%) worked in commerce and services in 1980, about 50% of its artesans and own—account workers, 85% of its petty—bourgeois owners and just over 30% (6.0% out of 19.9%) of its salaried petty bourgeoisie. Further, 100% of the category 'unemployed, subemployed and domestics' are classified as being in commerce and services, though this classification is certainly open to more doubt.

Putting all this together, we are now in a position to relate the geographical distribution of social classes, and their different degrees of concentration within Managua, to the functions which they perform within the national economy. It seems clear, for instance, that the strong concentration of the salaried middle class in the capital is due above all to the dominance of the city, first in

78

commerce and services, and second in central government. There is also
an element which is due to the concentration in Managua of 'non-
productive' workers within manufacturing industry. This is apparent
from table 5.7, but it can also be seen there that the small degree of
concentration which there is is entirely a result of the spatial
organisation of the food, drink and tobacco industry. More generally,
the concentration of the salaried petty bourgeoisie within Managua
seems to be very little due to the internal organisation of
manufacturing industry and very much more to do with the centralisation
in the city of the commercial and service sectors, and of the central
government.

Table 5.7
PRODUCTIVE WORKERS AS A % OF TOTAL
NICARAGUA AND MANAGUA[1]

	1980		1981		1982		1983	
Sector	N	M	N	M	N	M	N	M
Food, drink, tobacco	65	45	67	50	63	48	60	48
Textiles	81	82	87	81	78	79	77	78
Wood	80	83	76	77	71	71	68	67
Paper	48	46	61	60	64	62	54	53
Chemicals + petroleum	60	64	64	64	57	57	57	58
Minerals	71	71	72	73	70	70	75	76
Metal-working	82	82	86	86	71	71	75	75
Machinery	70	70	75	79	64	67	74	73
Others	64	64	62	62	64	64	65	64
TOTAL	67	64	70	61	66	61	?	?

Source: MIND; INEC.

[1] Region III: i.e. wider than the city of Managua

The picture of Managua as the centre of industrial production is far
less clear. Less than a quarter (23.9%) of Managua's total
economically-active population is engaged in sectors of 'material

79

production'. These sectors account for about half of artesanal and own-account workers, and about 40% of the proletariat. In other words although the proletariat as a class shows a degree of concentration in Managua (see above) less than half of it in the city is engaged in material production (or just about half if a proportion of state workers is included). From the data available it is unfortunately difficult to get a sense of how this compares with the rest of Nicaragua. If the percentage employed in 'material production' in Managua (23.9%) is compared with estimates for national employment in 'secondary production' (manufacturing plus construction), Managua comes out ahead: the national figures are 19.5% for 1978 (CIERA-UNRISD, 1984, p.58) and 15% for 1984 (INETER-MINVAH). On the other hand, a sample household survey (INEC, 1982) showed Managua to have a lower proportion of non-agroprocessing industrial workers than other urban areas.

Managua, then, is clearly a centre of non-agricultural material production but possibly not the overwhelmingly-dominant centre. It is the centre of factory-production of consumer goods and of that manufacturing industry, much of it owned by foreign capital or by Somoza, which was introduced in the period of the Alliance for Progress and the Central American Common Market. This is the industry more related to the 'new international division of labour'. It stretches round the shores of Lake Managua on either side of the city and out along the road from Managua to the airport. But there is also in Nicaragua agro-industrial production associated with its position within the 'old international division of labour'. These industries are for the minimal processing required by exports even of primary commodities. So one of the biggest concentrations in the country of a classic industrial proletariat (and one which has been active and important politically) is in the sugar refineries near Chinandega. Similarly, though on a smaller scale, south of Matagalpa there are the 'beneficios' for the coffee grown in the hills to the north, and in the region around León a scattering of cotton gins. Further, as was seen in chapter 3, the early emphasis on big agro-industrial projects would have increased this presence of a factory proletariat outside of the capital city.

So is Managua unproductive? What can be said about characterisation of Managua, mentioned in chapter 4, as the parasitic blot on the landscape of the productive countryside?

Certainly in terms of some definitions of the productive/non-productive distinction, Managua would seem to live up to its image. The fact that less than a quarter of its workforce work in sectors of 'material production' is one obvious potential criterion. Moreover, although as we have seen there are data difficulties in comparing this with the national average, it does seem to be clear that Managua has a higher proportion of commerce and services. Nor, as we have also seen, does the relatively large presence of a proletariat in the city imply an equivalent importance of material production. This is even more true of the 'middle classes'. From table 5.6 it can be calculated that as many middle class people in Managua work in commerce and services (13% of the economically active population = 7.0% of the petty-bourgeois owners and 6.0% of the salaried petty bourgeoisie) as members of the proletariat, and that this represents an even stronger proportional concentration of these groups into these sectors. Moreover, where the data on this relatively high level of commerce and services, and low level of material production, is questionable is precisely where it relates to assumptions about the nature of the 'informal sector'. As has been argued, on the one hand, it is undoubtedly suspect to classify all of the 'subemployed' in commerce and services, while on the other hand much clearly unproductive informal-sector buying and selling is done by middle-class people who also have formal-sector jobs, and it is the latter by which they would be classified in table 5.6.

But all of this, of course, implies accepting a distinction between 'productive' and 'unproductive' based around the presence or absence of material production. This is a definition often used in Nicaragua, and implicitly in many other debates, but it is clearly open to question (and indeed has been much questioned). In one sense it does have the merit of not following that definition of productive which confines it to activities generative of surplus value. Such a definition may be applicable to purely capitalist societies (or perhaps more specifically to a capitalist mode of production) but would certainly not be relevant to a Sandinista strategy for an economy and society in transition. This is the crux of the matter. For any meaningful definition must be based on some notion of what is necessary for the reproduction of society and of the social project, including but not restricted to, the macro-economic equations which have to be

satisfied. There are therefore, for example, many activities outside
of material production which are clearly productive in the sense of
being essential to the Sandinista project.[2] The definition in this
sense must always be society-specific or politically-specific, a
position argued strongly in the Nicaraguan context by Corragio (1984).
Thus in relation particularly to Nicaragua, Corragio argues that 'The
commercial and financial systems - most especially in a society which
has chosen circulation as the sphere through which to capture the
surplus - must be seen as involving labour which is necessary to the
social management of the economy' (translation). Part of Managua's
reputation as 'unproductive' and 'parasitic' comes from the previous
location there of the financial and commercial strata. Yet the city is
no longer the seat of this previously-dominant part of the private
sector. The Sandinista strategy thus far has precisely been to
eliminate unproductive capitalist elements in the city and unproductive
uncapitalist owners in the countryside. This has had two effects: it
has reinforced the production-orientation of the countryside and it has
made central to the political project of transition (and therefore in
Corragio's terms potentially 'productive') some of the functions of the
previously parasitic strata. This is an issue which we shall pick up
again, precisely in its specific political context, in the next
chapter.

Footnotes

1   The term is actually 'no-agropecuario'. It is not clear how
     the division was made. It will clearly bear some relation to,
     though it is not the same as, the distinction between urban and
     rural. In what follows the terms are used interchangeably, but
     the distinction should be borne in mind. Since most of the
     comparisons are anyway between the national total and the
     figures for Managua, the analysis should be unaffected.

2   The data is therefore from the start clearly inadequate since
     it refers only to paid labour. Much necessary labour, in this
     sense, goes unpaid.

CHAPTER 6 : A SOCIO-SPATIAL CONTRADICTION

The strategy of survival

Although, as we said, much of the analysis in the last chapter had
necessarily to be based on data which is now a few years old, all the
indications are that its conclusions will if anything have been
reinforced in subsequent years. The process of migration to Managua
from the countryside seems to have continued. There was some
decentralisation of state functions in 1982 (see next chapter) but as
far as it is possible to tell this does not seem to have brought with
it much geographical decentralisation of personnel. Moreover in the
last two years some of these characteristics of the capital city and of
its evolving role within the country as a whole have increasingly come
to be seen as problematical. This is in part because of the inexorable
continuation of some of the processes themselves. But it is also
because the processes are made more problematical by a shift which has
taken place in national economic strategy.

Up until 1983 the economic strategy outlined in chapter 3, that of
concentrating on major projects and on improving the agro-export base
of the economy (the Strategy of Reconstruction), had a creditable
degree of success in national economic terms. This is certainly true

83

if the performance of the Nicaraguan economy is compared with that of other Central American countries. Increasingly, however, the strategy began to run into trouble. The reason for this lay in a conjunction of long-term changes and more immediate problems. Firstly, the underlying long-term weakness of an economic model which relies for its insertion into the international capitalist market on the export of primary commodities was brought home hard in the early 1980s. In only the first four years of that decade the terms of trade for Nicaragua's main exports declined by 30%. In part this was a reflection of a long-term underlying tendency, but it was also, secondly, exacerbated by the impact of world recession. All the economies of the Central American region were rocking and were only being kept afloat by massive injections, in one form or another, of aid from the USA. Nicaragua, in total contrast, was beginning to feel the effects of an economic blockade imposed by the United States. A further, critical, 'conjunctural' factor was the war of aggression, again financed and promoted by the USA. The effects of the war on the economy showed up in numerous ways. Most simply, it absorbed (and continues to absorb) about half of annual government expenditure and something like a quarter of GNP. This is an enormous drain on a country with an already weak and dependent economy and which is struggling not simply to reproduce that economy but also to improve living standards for the majority of its people and to pursue quite fundamental changes in social organisation. In this context, the aggression against Nicaragua is costly not only in terms of vital and scarce financial resources, but also in terms of labour power. At any one time something like 100,000 people are unavailable for work because they are involved directly in defence. This worsens an already-existing shortage of labour which is particularly acute in the countryside – a subject to which we shall return. The situation is even worse in the case of people with administrative and technical skills. Such skills are very scarce in Nicaragua, in part because there was so little training and education under Somoza, in part because some of the relatively advantaged people who did have such skills left for Miami and other such places after July 1979. The war is therefore costly in taking from the needs of production and of the administration of the economy people whose skills are vitally needed in those sectors.

The war is also quite explicitly <u>directed at</u> the economy. Many of the targets are not military. There are constant attacks on economic targets: on coffee pickers and coffee harvests, on tobacco fields and tobacco-drying sheds, on production cooperatives. Attacks such as these can have much more than the obvious reverberative effects on the economy. There were no big attacks on coffee-harvesters in 1986, for example, and coffee prices were high that year. But the coffee harvest was not as big as it might have been - because there <u>had</u> been attacks the year before and some of the coffee had been left unpicked, and coffee bushes, to produce good yields, need to be picked every year...

Moreover even only sporadic attacks increase the costs of production, and make production more difficult, in quite large regions of the country, in the south along the Costa Rican border and most especially in the north and centre. This has affected both cattle-ranching, in the south, and the production of basic foods, in the north. It has also necessitated vast programmes of geographical reorganisation in the affected regions, in particular involving peasantry living in isolated areas moving into more clustered newly-built settlements. It is estimated that something like one tenth of the population of the country will have been involved in some such movement by the time the current programmes are complete. Finally, all this in its turn, as was seen in chapter 5, can only increase the migratory flows from the countryside to the city.

Thus, a combination of the change in the terms of trade, the impact of the world recession which among other things reinforced the worsening in the terms of trade, the US boycott and the war served to make Nicaragua's economic position increasingly precarious. Not only was it more difficult to survive internationally on the basis of existing export crops but the food situation within the country was also becoming more difficult. In part this latter situation resulted from the effects of the war, mentioned above. In part it also resulted from Sandinista policies. An important element of policy since 1979 has, as was mentioned in chapter 3, been to increase the availability of food to the mass of the population. Apart from retaining in the country some food which had previously been exported, peasants were granted very large amounts of credit to increase and improve production. Systems of shops were established, run by the state in the countryside, selected by local neighbourhood committees in the towns.

Perhaps most important of all, food prices were heavily subsidised. All this, however, had contradictory effects. Low prices discouraged production in some cases; for instance on large state farms where basic grains would have been grown for the workers it became cheaper to buy food in. Such problems of production, moreover, occurred in a context where demand for food, precisely as one of the successes of the revolution, was increasing fast. The report 'Managua is Nicaragua' documents in detail how the post-79 period has witnessed an increased demand for food — by the virtual elimination of malnutrition, by increasing demand for food beyond the absolute basics, and by population growth. It is, however, an increased demand which is proving more and more difficult to meet and this in turn provokes further reverberations through the structure of the economy. It leads to increased imports of food and of raw inputs for food production. It thereby increases the need to export, and exacerbates the financial pressure on the system as a whole. It increases external dependence. Moreover, since these problems mean that it is in fact impossible to import sufficient food to meet demand, the supply of food remains low relative to demand. This in turn, and in spite of all the formalities of the distribution system, opens the door to the 'informal' commercial sector to make a killing out of shortages. This opportunity potentially attracts more people to it, thus reducing still further the labour available for production. This, anyway, is the argument of the highly detailed report produced by CIERA - MIDINRA (1984, see for instance p.213). It was in this context that the shift in the emphasis of national economic strategy took place towards what was to be called 'The Strategy of Survival'.

The focus of the Strategy of Survival is exactly as its name implies. The emphasis is shifted even more to the production of food, with the aim of at least sitting it out until the war is over. In class terms it means prioritising the peasantry. This is true _within_ the countryside where the emphasis is shifting away from big investment projects and export crops towards smallholdings and the production of basic grains, especially maize and beans. It is also true in terms of the distribution of resources _between_ town and countryside. Geographically the priority is the countryside. There is therefore little investment available for urban areas, and certainly not for Managua.

Contradictory processes

In the context of this strategy, many of the socio-spatial characteristics and processes discussed in chapter 5 are deeply problematical.

A continuing high rate of urbanisation is clearly contradictory with a national economic strategy which aims to maximise labour-intensive smallholder food production in the countryside. The fact that at least some part of this faster growth of the cities, and especially of Managua, seems to be taking place through migration, and specifically through rural-urban migration, is particularly problematical. As has been said, there is a shortage of labour in the countryside. In part this is as a direct result of the war taking workers generally. In part it is because migrant labourers, who used to come over the border from Honduras, no longer do so. It is also in part another example of a gain of the revolution having contradictory effects. Members of what in table 5.5 is classified as the rural semi-proletariat, very poor peasants, who in the past would have to supplement their incomes through wage earning by working others' land, are now no longer under such pressure to do so because of the considerable improvement in the living standards of much of the peasantry since the revolution. In terms of class changes this means some shift from the semi-proletariat to the peasantry. In terms of the general availability of wage-labour in the countryside, its effects are clearly negative. In terms of the production of food it is more ambiguous.

But if in this way there has been some growth in the size of the peasantry, one nonetheless hears, more widely, foreboding tales of the 'autodestruction' of that class. This is where the link to urbanisation and migration is made. Probably the main reason for the preoccupation with migration to Managua is that migration is equated with rural-urban migration and that in turn to class changes, from peasantry to urban working class and specifically, it is assumed, to the urban informal sector which in turn is defined as unproductive. This analysis is current not only in political and policy-making circles, and in the popular media, in Nicaragua, but also in most academic interpretations of the situation. Thus, Harris, 1985:

'The occupational structure of Managua reveals that productive wage-earners represent a <u>declining</u> proportion of the city's total labour force. In 1963, wage-earners involved in productive economic activity - manufacturing, construction, utilities, etc. - accounted for one third of the total employed population, whereas by 1982 this sector had declined to less than one-quarter. In other words, the growth of the urban population in Nicaragua's most important cities - now at a rate of 6 per cent per annum - has <u>not</u> contributed to the creation of a modern industrial working class, permanently installed in large industrial establishments. The contingents of rural migrants to the cities generally find employment only in the so-called informal sector. In Managua, this 'informal sector' of self-employed pedlars, handymen and artesans without formal wage-earning employment represents approximately 45 per cent of the economically active population.'

Much of what is said in this quotation is perfectly correct. It is true that wage-earners in manufacturing, construction and utilities have declined in relative importance in Managua over the last two decades. It is true that the 'so-called informal sector' has grown enormously, both absolutely and relatively. It is true that many migrants from the countryside probably went into the informal sector to earn a living. With the lack of industrial employment before the revolution and the relative attractiveness of some parts of the informal sector subsequently there was, indeed, little else people could do. Finally it is true that there is a very low level of development of a 'modern industrial working class', particularly if that is defined as 'permanently installed in large industrial establishments', in Managua and indeed in Nicaragua as a whole.

But the passage also contains some common, but misconceived, equations. Productive wage-earners are simply defined as belonging to three sectors, so making a tangible good is productive, however useless that commodity in the reproduction of Nicaraguan society, while selling tortillas (even through a formal enterprise) is not. Further, while there is an explicit equation between (productive) formal-sector wage-earners and working class, which as we have seen Vilas (1984)

88

would question, there is also an implicit equation between formal-sector wage-earning, in specified sectors, and productive work. The informal sector, which also contains manufacturing, construction and utilities, is apparently not only not working class but also unproductive. Finally, and relatedly, while it is clear that few rural migrants went into formal-sector manufacturing, it is not clear that all of them went into the informal sector. Many must also have gone into the fast-growing commercial and services branches which are part of the formal sector.

So what has been happening? Again there are limitations of data, but some things can be discerned. It is clear, to begin with, that the tertiary sector has grown markedly in Nicaragua as a whole over recent decades. This is shown in table 6.1. Further, as table 5.7 showed for recent years, there has also been some growth of 'service' employment within the secondary sector of the economy.

Table 6.1
SECTORS OF THE ECONOMY (NICARAGUA)
(% OF EMPLOYMENT)

	1950	1960	1970	1978	1984
Primary sector	67.7	59.6	46.6	42.1	35
Secondary sector	15.0	15.9	16.3	19.5	15
manufacturing	11.4	11.7	12.0	15.0	
construction	3.6	4.2	4.3	4.3	
Tertiary sector	17.3	24.5	37.3	45.0	50
Commerce	6.1	8.3	9.6	12.8	
Other	11.2	16.2	27.7	32.2	

Source: CIERA-UNRISD, 1984, p 58. 1984 figures : INETER-MINVAH

There has also been over the long term a marked growth in the sector defined as informal. Table 6.2 gives some indication of this.

Table 6.2
NICARAGUA: DISTRIBUTION OF ECONOMICALLY ACTIVE POPULATION (%)

	1950	1960	1970	1980
Urban sector	30.3	37.2	47.5	57.8
formal	18.6	22.1	26.8	29.5
informal	6.5	9.1	12.6	17.6
domestic service	5.2	6.0	8.1	10.7
Agricultural sector	68.8	62.0	51.9	41.8
modern	42.9	33.5	25.9	18.0
traditionally	25.9	28.5	26.0	23.8
Mining	0.9	0.9	0.6	0.4

Source: PREALC. Mercado de Trabajo en Cifras, 1950–1980 cited in CIERA–UNRISD, 1984, p.27.

Moreover in Managua these processes have been more marked than in the country as a whole. Table 6.3 shows the long–term shifts in the city between productive and non–productive and salaried and non–salaried workers. Table 6.4 shows the importance of the informal sector in Managua in 1982.

These are the tables used by Harris in his analysis quoted above, and there are a number of things to note about them. First of all, no detailed definitions of categories are given in the tables, and in respect of both the absolute numbers in table 6.3 and the percentages in both tables they are hard to square with the categories used in table 5.6. This is not to say that these tables are wrong, but to point out that they are very difficult to interpret. Harris' working class is the salaried productive working class of table 6.3, but it is also clear that there are both other salaried workers (44.6% of the

90

economically-active) and other productive workers (9.4%). Nor is it clear how these definitions relate to the definition of the informal sector in table 6.4, when table 6.3 indicates a total of 68.7% of the city's workers being salaried in 1982.

Table 6.3

OCCUPATIONAL STRUCTURE OF THE CITY OF MANAGUA (%)

	1963	1976	1980	1981	1982
Productive and salaried	33.3	28.4	24.3	27.0	24.1
Productive/ non-salaried	11.2	8.0	10.5	11.7	9.4
Unproductive/ salaried	41.2	48.8	40.0	42.9	44.6
Unproductive/ unsalaried	14.3	14.8	25.2	18.4	21.9
	100.0	100.0	100.0	100.0	100.0
(in thousands)	(74.2)	(158.8)	(164.2)	(186.5)	(203.2)

Source: Barricada, Lunes Socioeconómico, 2.1.1984

Table 6.4

OCCUPATIONAL COMPOSITION OF THE CITY OF MANAGUA IN 1982 (%)

Informal sector	45.6
Salaried industrial	12.5
Formal commercial and service sector	33.2
Non-salaried industrial	5.6
Other	3.1
	100.0

Source: Barricada, Lunes socioeconómico, 2.1.1984

91

None of this, again, is to question the overall line of argument but it is to point to problems of conceptualisation. The issue here is the 'productiveness' of the economic and social structure. It is clear that Managua, within Nicaragua, is a centre of sectors outside of material production, and in particular that is a centre of commerce and services. But as was argued in chapter 5, it is not clear that this is necessarily an appropriate way of characterising what is unproductive employment. Still less is it clear that the whole of the informal sector should be classified as unproductive. This is true, as was pointed out in chapter 4, even in the sense of material production. Table 4.1 showed, for instance, that in 1982 19% of informal-sector jobs in Nicaragua and 16.2% in Managua, were in manufacturing (though it is interesting that the figure is lower for Managua than for the country as a whole, as it is also (obviously) for the category 'agriculture, hunting and fishing', the difference being made up by commerce and services). More fundamentally, the definition of the informal sector is based primarily on the social relations of production and size of enterprise, rather than on anything related to notions of productiveness.

In the current situation in Nicaragua, and with the current economic strategy of survival, Managua's unproductiveness in fact is defined overwhelmingly, in the policy debate, in relation to the production of food. It does not produce food, or not very much; on the contrary it consumes a large amount; further, the amount consumed per head is probably higher than in the rest of the country given the concentration in the city of higher-income people; and these two last points - the concentration together of so many consumers and particularly of consumers who can afford to pay more - encourages the development of speculative trading which in turn results in higher prices. Put this together with the severe shortage of producers in the countryside, and it is clear that the high level and rate of urbanisation within Nicaragua is contradictory with the prevailing economic strategy. The specifically spatial form of Nicaraguan society (the high degree and the nature of the concentration in Managua) is having its own effects on the potential for developing certain kinds of economic strategies. CIERA-UNRISD (1984) argues that to increase food security requires above all a transformation of the relations between

92

Managua and the rest of the country, between city and countryside, and between worker and peasant (p.213).

However, it is not particularly the working class of Managua, even widely defined, which is not in this sense 'productive'. Still less is it those primarily working in the informal sector or those living in new spontaneous settlements. Indeed these last two groups probably produce more food than most. It is also the middle class which is in this sense 'unproductive', and as was seen in chapter 5 this class is concentrated in Managua more than any other. The problem is rarely interpreted in relation to the middle class, however, since this group although as far as one can tell including a significant proportion of migrants, does not form an important component of rural–urban migration (see chapter 5). Rather, they tend to arrive in Managua from other cities. Neither, and this is important in terms of the policy–debate, is there much chance of them ever decentralising to the countryside to grow food.

But, as we saw in chapter 4, neither are the majority of people on the new spontaneous settlements recently–arrived rural migrants. No more than the middle class are they on the whole likely to convert themselves overnight into campesinos. Moreover, as we saw in chapter 5, middle–class migration can be an axis around which turns a wider process of migration, including migration from the countryside. And as we have also seen, the spatial concentration of higher–income groups in Managua is an important stimulus to the growth of 'informal–sector' speculative trading.

The middle class is also important in another sense. While the need to produce food in the context of the strategy of survival is a prime aspect of the contradiction between high rates of urbanisation and the current economic policy, there are also other aspects. Chief among these are the problems of the overburdened infrastructure of Managua (chapter 4) and the consequently high costs of accommodating more growth, particularly in a context, again, where it has been decided that the overwhelming priority for new investment must be the countryside. Yet while the new spontaneous settlements are the most visible sign of the continued expansion of the city, at least spatially, and while newspaper articles alongside pictures of new settlements write ominously of the impossible strains on the city's infrastructure, in per capita terms it is the middle class, not the new settlers, who put the strain on the city's supplies. Precise figures are not available but it seems unlikely that those living on new settlements, with a couple of light-bulbs' worth of illegally-tapped electricity each, and water from pumps, can use as much of either as those in the bungalows of Pancasán who each morning water their gardens and hose down their cars. If the spontaneous settlements do pose a specific problem in relation to infrastructure and the use of resources, this results precisely from the fact that they are unplanned. On the one hand this means that their location does not necessarily bear any sensible relation to available supply. On the other hand on the settlements where water and electricity are taken illegally no payment can even be collected for its use.

All this leaves the Sandinistas with a huge quandary, which has both spatial and class dimensions. Chapters 3 and 5 analysed some of the socio-spatial characteristics of Nicaragua and some of the major changes currently under way, including those resulting from the revolutionary process itself and from the initial economic strategy of reconstruction. This chapter has begun to document the subsequent need to move from the strategy of reconstruction to a strategy of survival. The problem is that this new economic strategy requires a reworking of socio-spatial relations including a restraint on, if not a reversal of, some of the dominant current processes of change. On its own, however, the economic strategy itself will not produce those spatial changes. The question then is how to intervene in the socio-spatial changes going on intra-nationally in order to make feasible the national economic strategy. Yet on all sides, given the desperate lack of resources, there are problems.

Take first the middle class. As we have just argued, its concentration in Managua is undoubtedly key, and clearly problematical. The image which their presence gives the city, together with the functions they perform, in the state and the headquarters of commercial and mass organisations, are the basis of Managua's hegemony over the rest of the country. The indications are that their presence generates further migration, that they use more resources than others, and so forth.

But there is also no doubt that the middle class on the whole does not want to leave Managua. In the current stage, moreover, the Sandinistas are wary of alienating them too much; the shortage of

94

administrative and technical labour is too acute, and at an individual level – although as a group it has probably grown – their standard of living has undoubtedly already fallen a lot. Moreover the incredible lack of infrastructure <u>outside</u> Managua means that it is currently very difficult to envisage any serious geographical decentralisation of state functions (although some attempt was made in 1982). There clearly is <u>some</u> potential. The need to decentralise the higher education system to other towns is often spoken of, for instance. Yet here too there are problems. A recent foreign-aid package for the university stipulated that the new department to be funded should be in Managua because it was the most prestigious campus. Meanwhile, however, the general strategy of prioritizing the countryside and investing as little as possible in Managua means that living conditions in the capital anyway continue to deteriorate, even for the middle class.

But they are far worse, and also deteriorating, for the popular classes of Managua. Particularly this is true for those living on still-unrecognised spontaneous settlements. Here, the situation is compounded by the lack of security from not having formal ownership rights. Moreover, as was established in chapter 4, these people are not recent migrants from the countryside but in the majority Managuans squeezed out by the desperate shortage of housing in the city. As such, they are the people who began this story, whose insurrection in the final days assured the success of the revolution, and of the Sandinistas. Their expectations, reinforced by the experience of the first years after 1979, are high. But they are expectations which, if the strategy is to prioritise the countryside, cannot be fulfilled. So conditions worsen, and discontent begins to grow. Although as yet it does not seem to be on any major scale, this is fertile ground for organisation against the Sandinistas by their enemies, both to the left and to the right.

Yet conditions are often objectively as bad if not worse for the peasantry in the countryside, especially the poorer peasantry. If they are to remain in the countryside, producing the food which is central to the strategy of survival, it is their conditions which must be improved. There is, moreover, a further huge difference between Managua and the rest of the country, or at least large parts of the countryside. The war; which sometimes in Managua hardly seems to exist

95

except in the newpapers and in the visibility of the army on the streets, but which in some regions of the countryside is an everyday reality. The war is indeed both an element in the need to produce more food, and an autonomous reason for prioritising the peasantry as a class. For it is the peasantry which is on the front line against the contra.

CHAPTER 7 : NEW POLICIES

Agrarian Reform: a new stage

From 1984 onwards the amount of land distributed to smallholders, whether organised individually or in cooperatives, began to increase dramatically (Fauné, 1986, p.23) partly in response to increasingly vociferous demands by the people of the countryside themselves. By early 1986 a new stage in the Agrarian Reform programme was announced. It represented a number of important changes from previous stages. Most importantly the criteria for land liable to takeover were extended. Now farming the land up to its productive potential, in whatever crop was being grown, was no longer a guarantee against reform.For it could be, argued the new legislation, that the land could nonetheless be better used when broken up into smallholdings for the production of maize and beans. If the first stage of the Agrarian Reform was, in terms of the criteria for the land affected, simply anti-Somocista, and the second stage 'productive capitalist' in that production was sufficient to guarantee immunity from reform, this stage is arguing that efficiency on capitalist criteria may not any longer in itself be sufficient; that there may be other, social, criteria of efficiency in the use of land, and that these may prevail. This is not an entirely new line of argument in the agrarian reform; it had been used in particular, special circumstances before (moreover, on similar lines there already existed credit restrictions on which crops individual farmers could grow), but it was now fully integrated as part of the reform. Further, the maximum size of holding over which estates came within the remit of the agrarian reform was reduced.

This was all within the private sector. A further new element of this stage of the agrarian reform was a reversal of previous policy, in that state holdings were also reduced. Land from state farms is being divided up and distributed. In part this shift in policy was a response to pressure of demand by the peasantry, but it was also in recognition of the problems being experienced by some state farms. And in turn these problems resulted in part from the shortage of administrative and technical workers which has already been mentioned.

In this stage of the reform, then, most of the new holdings created are being given to the peasantry, or, rather, the peasantry is being expanded as land is given to the rural landless and to those whose landholdings were too small to survive on. The bulk of the land is being distributed to individual families, the rest as cooperatives. Within the cooperatives the effective labour force is being increased by encouraging the membership of more members of the family, rather than just the one member as had been normal in the past. The dominance of the individual basis of distribution is again a response to expressed demand, a form of demand itself reinforced by the fact that cooperatives are a particularly favoured target of the contra. There has thus been a shift, in the different stages of land reform, not only in the criteria for takeover (Somocista; unproductive; social criteria) but also in the form of redistribution, with the state being most important in the first stage, cooperatives in the second, and individual farmers in the third. UNAG supports this shift as a response to immediate demands but in the longer term would like to see increased cooperativisation.

All of this is a clear response, first to the need to produce more food (transferring land from the large-private and state sectors involves a parallel shift from export crops to basic grains); that is it is part of the strategy of survival. Second, it is a response to the war and to the need to consolidate the peasantry as a base, and third it is a response to the need to hold people in the countryside and stem the rate of urbanisation which might undermine the strategy of survival.

There have been other recent measures, too, designed towards the same ends and in particular towards the last. There have been changes in the systems of food pricing and distribution. Producers of maize and beans in the war zones can now sell to whomever they want; they are no longer formally restricted to the official channels, from which anyway much production was always held back for sale at far higher prices to buyers for the informal commercial sector. More generally, sales within regions are now unrestricted, and state and private systems of purchase and distribution are recognised to exist side by side. The prices the state system pays to producers have also been raised and subsidies ended on the price of basic grains. All of this group of measures is designed both to encourage more production by raising (official) returns and at the same time to attract more of the produce back to the official channels by increasing its price-competitiveness with the informal-sector buyers. In fact, however, the evidence is that the price-differential is still very considerable. Indeed while there remains a shortage of such basic goods – that is, until the problem of increasing production has been solved – unofficial buyers will almost always be able to attract sales through paying higher prices. To make this more difficult, other restraints have been retained, or newly imposed, on distribution systems. In a clear recognition that the problem is focussed on the potential market, and profit, in Managua, while intra-regional sales have been freed-up, inter-regional sales are still formally restricted to official channels. The aim is to prevent food finding its way to Managua. To back this up there are currently frequent searches of buses and trucks coming into Managua from outside. Moreover the huge Mercado Oriental within the city has been reorganised in an effort to restrict it more to direct sellers, and in local communities people are being encouraged to do their own price-checks. On top of this, within the official system of distribution, the countryside gets priority and Managua comes last. Within this system any shortages are felt first in Managua. The prioritisation of the countryside is designed to increase the quality of life there in comparison with that in Managua and to reduce thereby the attraction of migration to the city. The irony of course is that the resultant shortages in Managua further increase the attractiveness of the city as a magnet for the informal sector and therefore increase in turn the need for a clamp-down on that sector.

All this is going on, as we have said, in the context of a shift of overall investment from town to country and from large projects to small. There are also, within the quite debilitating resource-constraints, active development programmes in regions outside Managua, for instance a flourishing and progressive programme of cooperatives (much of it having to be funded on an individual-project basis from outside Nicaragua) in the region of Matagalpa. Other measures are also being taken to increase production. New production norms have been negotiated in workplaces and there is a big emphasis on increasing productivity. Enticements to work in the formal sector have been increased. State farms are being encouraged to grow the food-supplies for their own workers (a practice which had declined when subsidised prices meant that it was cheaper to buy food off the farm); even the army is growing food for itself.

One of the aims of this range of measures is to increase the relative attractiveness of the countryside and reduce the drift to Managua. It remains to be seen whether it will have this effect. It will, however, alter some of the spatial characteristics and relationships discussed in chapters 3 and 5. The 'ownership' characteristic of the countryside will be reinforced both through the expansion of the peasantry and the parallel decline of semi- and sub-proletariats as people are given sufficient land, and through the reduction in the proletariat with the cutback in the state sector. On the latter, indeed, the policies mark a significant shift from the view of the state's role as a dominant axis of social and economic development in the countryside. The political emphasis now is very much on the peasantry and on the peasants' union UNAG. Within this context, one aim nevertheless is for the state sector to play a coordinating role and to develop better links with the peasant producers in their areas. In the case of some state farms there are plans not only for the distribution of some of their land to small-scale producers, but also for an element of the state farm to remain as a central supplier of communal services, including in some cases labour for particular tasks.

The measures should also reduce somewhat the degree to which agricultural production in the countryside is formally tied into and dominated by controls emanating from Managua. The changes in the food distribution systems reduce the degree of formal control from that direction by the state, over sales by the sector which is growing most in the countryside – the peasantry. Moreover the attempt to control the non-formal distribution channels between regions is in an effort to prevent state dominance from Managua simply being replaced by effective dominance through the speculative market focussed on the city. Meanwhile, the sector with the most direct relationship back to Managua, the state sector, is in relative decline as a direct producer in the countryside. Overall it would seem that this group of measures, linked in to the economic strategy of survival, might in comparison with the effect of the economic strategy of reconstruction in the early years, tend to reduce a little the structural dominance of Managua over the rest of the country.

In Managua itself the effect is further to worsen living conditions. The low priority of Managua for general investment, its low priority in terms of food distribution, and the rise in food prices, all make living in the capital city even more of a struggle. In a way, of course, this is the effect intended, but in this part of the country, furthest removed from the war, where the causes of shortage are least obvious, it is most likely to breed political discontent.

Planning Managua

Meanwhile within Managua itself the policy debate continues. In 1982 there was a measure of decentralisation of the functions of the state. This took place, in other words, after the date of the statistics in table 5.6. However it seems that it did not lead to any major change in the balance of workers between Managua and the rest of the country. (This is also indicated by the later figures from INEC, but again these are still only for 1982, the year in which the decentralisation took place.) There have been, and are in process of being drawn up, a number of plans for the city. And a number of different bodies – the Alcaldía, MINVAH and the government of Region III – are centrally concerned with the issue of what to do about Managua.

One of the fundamental background issues concerns the very definition of urban and rural. Always given the fact that there is no clear and generally accepted definition of either term, Managua is a very unurban city. The discontinuous scatter of the built-up area, the patches of agricultural production, the subsistence production on some of the settlements, the cows which occasionally make you swerve the car suddenly in the middle of town... To look at, Managua offers enormous possibilities for breaking down the urban-rural distinction by ruralising the urban. A strategy of agricultural development within Managua could not only turn to advantage the current pattern of the built-up area but also reduce the parasitic character of the city in terms of food production. Things, however, are rarely that simple. For one thing, agricultural production would place huge extra demands on the already inadequate water supply. For another, retaining the current pattern of scattered urban development is more costly in terms of the provision of infrastructure, such as electricity and water, than is concentrating whatever new growth is allowed in the currently empty areas in the city's structure. Finally, the dominant planning concepts used, for instance in the housing ministry, tend to be of the rather standard and geometrical sort with the temptation always being first to draw a line round the city precisely to delimit it, and differentiate it from rural areas. So most of the plans for Managua over the long term locate new development in the interstices (see chapter 4). And in spite of the constant criticism of the unproductive nature of the city, there was a pronouncement in early 1986 banning cows from Managua.

But a pronouncement is one thing, and implementation is another. There still seem to be as many cows in Managua as before. Moreover there are elements of policy which do tend in the opposite direction. In particular, the physical nature of the area in which Managua is located makes it highly risky if not impossible to have continuous urban development. Many areas are crossed by fault lines vulnerable to seismic activity; the memory of the earthquake of 1972 is still very close. And the strip of land to the north of the city, along the lake, is vulnerable to flooding. Some of the open areas are to be used as recreational open space. Others, it is planned, will be planted with trees. Others, however, will be developed for agricultural use. Indeed there have already been a number of advances in this direction. South of the central area of town, but north of the large Plaza 19 de julio, there is a considerable area of irrigated agricultural development. Between the Primavera barrio and the lake, to the north east of the city, there is a flourishing agricultural cooperative.

A regional market garden (for Region III — Managua). This is within the city, just north of the Plaza 19th of July. The slogan says 'Let's all go and sow the land'.

Cooperativa José Alberto
Martínez Ugarte

'Our Cooperative is named after Jose Alberto Martínez Ugarte, a friend from the barrio who was killed by the National Guard before the insurrection. The Coop was founded in 1980, and received its land free, since before the revolution it had been owned by Somocistas. Today the coop has five members, and produces a wide range of goods. It has hens, grows papaya, onions, yuca, beans and maize, and we rotate the crops between different parts of the land through the year. There is no irrigation, but we receive technical aid from MIDINRA (the Ministry of Agriculture)... and anyway we all come from families who came to Managua only a generation ago.

The coop started with a loan, but we have no difficulty now in turning in a regular profit. We don't even have to go out and sell. People from the barrio come here and buy everything we can produce.' (interview)

View through the coop's chicken run, north to Lake Managua (the coop is on the shores of the lake). Papaya in the foreground.

So most of the, rather hypothetical, plans for the medium-term future of Managua do in fact also include a commitment to at least some agricultural development in the city. Moreover, in spite of the sworn commitment to preventing further urbanisation all the plans also have to include a recognition that there will in fact be further growth of the city, both in terms of population and spatially. This would be true even if there were no migration. And given that the Sandinistas will not adopt either coercive measures, or control of residence or the labour market on the Cuban model, there in fact continues to be at least some in-migration. Some kind of growth does therefore have to be allowed for. The question is where and in what social form.

It is thus that the spontaneous settlements continue to be a focus of political debate. If there is to be growth, then it would be better to plan its location, but the distribution of the spontaneous settlements often bears little relation either to plans or to physical safety. In principle Managua is divided into ten zones, and the planning of basic services is done on this basis. Unplanned settlements therefore clearly break this equilibrium. Moreover, although life is certainly worse for many in the countryside and probably worse even for many still living in overcrowded conditions in older barrios, the poverty of the settlements, and especially their precariousness, is highly visible. They are new, continuously growing, and formally illegal. They are, moreover, or have been, foci of community organisation in attempts to legalise their very existence, and to get supplies, legal or illegal, of water and electricity. And the people who are doing this organising, living on the settlements, are as we saw in chapter 4, the working class (broadly defined) of Managua, the people who fought in the final insurrection, with their expectations still heightened by the fact of victory, and this taking of land now the only way to improve their living conditions in a situation where those conditions are in fact worsening through the political strategy of the very revolution itself. Moreover that political strategy, of prioritising the countryside, with its consequent lack of investment available for urban areas could imply a further worsening of the housing supply in Managua in the future and therefore the likelihood of further land-occupations.

It was in the context of the development of this quandary that the government began to take a less encouraging line towards spontaneous settlements. In 1983 they announced that no more settlements would be granted legal recognition. This, however, had no noticeable effect on would-be settlers. Settlements continued to be established; indeed as we have seen there was a burst of new ones in 1984 as people took advantage of the political situation, for this was election year. Moreover as in the case of Pantasma (chapter 4) the government was very reluctant to take any measures stronger than pleading with the new settlers. The regulations on land use, designed as part of the Urban Reform, were utterly inadequate in this kind of situation.

Two-and-a-half years later, in 1985-6, stronger measures were attempted. It was decided that certain settlements would have to be decentralised. Meetings were held, and the situation was explained and discussed,... the problems of Managua, the need to produce food in the countryside... People were then told they could not stay where they were, and were given options. There were two options in rural areas, with housing, land and jobs provided, and two in urban areas, again with housing and jobs guaranteed. All the locations were close to Managua, though outside the built-up area. It was not a success. People resented the move, complained - precisely as the analysis in chapter 4 would suggest - that they were not recently peasant stock and anyway (since there were urban options available) that they were from Managua, and they wanted to stay in Managua. It was strongly suspected that, with the government firmly opposed to introducing any measures of control, people would anyway drift back to Managua. It had been hoped that the first one or two small settlements where this approach was tried might be 'pilots' for a wider programme. In fact, it seems, the idea has been dropped.

So there continue to be in Managua numerous spontaneous settlements which remain 'unrecognised'. The people there have neither security of tenure on their plots of land nor, therefore, a firm basis on which to go and argue with the ministries for the provision of basic services. This situation is beginning to have political effects within the settlements themselves. Firstly, and most seriously for the programme of transition, it is reducing the impetus to organisation. If there really is no chance of winning legal recognition or of getting electricity and water, there is much less point in turning up regularly to your CDS meeting. A major focus of barrio-level CDS activity can therefore wither away. There is evidence of a decline in barrio-activities in this situation, and of people beginning to try to solve their problems on an individual basis (INIES, 1986, p.85). Since, as was seen in chapter 4, participation of people in the barrio CDS mass organisation was a central way in which they were involved, after 1979, in the wider processes of change, this is a serious matter. If a major function of the CDS is lost, it may decrease people's wider participation in its other functions.

Further, the situation has posed real problems for the CDS organisers themselves. Those working on the settlements themselves find a major part of the organisation's raison d'être being stifled by the impossibility, because of lack of resources for the city, of winning any victories. Their position is made more difficult by the fact that in this situation differences can easily arise between the various levels of the organisation. CDS representatives at settlement level put the case for the demands of the settlers whose elected representative they are. At higher levels, however, such as the zone, there may be more ambivalence since people living in the wider area may not be enthusiastic about the continued establishment of new settlements. This varies, but there is certainly very rarely open antagonism; people understand and have sympathy with the needs of the settlers, indeed the settlers are, as we have seen, most typically people from the zone itself, squeezed out of the impossibly-overcrowded existing housing conditions. At the level of the city as a whole, however, CDS representatives have on occasions taken a clear stance against new spontaneous settlements and have made clear statements to this effect. In part this is because they work at the level of the city as a whole and see 'its' problems. In part, too, however, it may be that members at this level are more likely to be Frente members, not through any bias in their selection but because the overwhelming majority of political activists in Nicaragua are pro-Frente. For this reason they frequently find themselves in sympathy with government policy, or at least more in sympathy with it than the CDS organiser down at settlement level who, though s/he may well understand the wider pressures lying behind government policy, still have their settlement's rights to security and services to fight for.

Finally and most obviously, the whole situation can lead to disenchantment among the new settlers both with the failure to gain much through their organisation into a CDS, and more directly with the ministries, particularly of energy and water, which are failing to provide them with services. As far as one can tell it has led to very little real antagonism towards the Sandinista government itself. At least people know they are no longer at gunpoint. What people seem most concerned about is security; they want to know that they will not get moved off 'their' land. Nonetheless, as we have seen, expectations have been raised and people want more. There is a basis of discontent about material shortages which is, though only to a small extent, being used as a basis for anti-government organisation, particularly by right-wing religious groups. More seriously for the government it is precisely this kind of demand, as was seen in chapter 2, which has historically been the basis of barrio organisation in Managua. And yet the government cannot simply respond with more resources; it is caught in the class-quandary outlined at the end of the last chapter, and between town and country, unable to answer all the, what it sees as legitimate, demands upon it and obliged because of the shortage of resources and decisions about the broader strategy of national economic development, to prioritize the peasantry, and the countryside.

A number of measures have been discussed and worked on which would both provide a way out of the dilemma and turn to positive advantage some of the characteristics of the existing situation. Most obviously, the settlements could be 'recognised' simply in the sense of the people being guaranteed security; in areas where there are physical dangers in having long-term housing, instead of being granted rights to that particular piece of land people would be guaranteed rights, at some point in the future, to relocation within Managua. This would respond to the most basic issue, which is simply security, without requiring investment. On the basis of this the currently 'illegal' tapping of water and electricity could be at least made safe, and charged for. Alongside these measures there is also discussion and experimentation about what the 'strategy of survival' might mean in the cities, and especially in Managua. Barrio councils are being set up, their establishment at the moment initially coordinated through the CDS, but including all other groups and mass organisations represented in the barrio. These councils are to organise 'survival' at barrio level, from painting buildings, to cleaning, to getting desks for the school, to mending walls. It is the council which organises, somehow or other, the acquisition of necessary resources (paint, wood...) and the people of the barrio who put in the labour. So far the response has been positive. Such a form of organisation can rebuild a sense of purpose and of collectivity, and it can put new life back into the CDS and other participating movements.

None of this means that the issue of the spontaneous settlements can easily be solved, either for the planners, or for the government, or for the settlers themselves. It could provide a major step forward; but as ever that itself, the improvement of conditions and so forth, could encourage the formation of yet more settlements...

Whatever happens, the new spontaneous settlements, and the people who live there, are likely to remain a central focus of political debate, in which the settlers themselves loudly participate. The settlers do not have the kind of coherence sometimes attributed to them: they are not all recent migrants from the countryside, they do not all work in the so-called 'informal sector'. But they are being converted into 'active subjects' in a political debate (INIES, 1986, p.78) which brings together and intertwines a whole number of threads of discussion. Managua is not the seat of unproductive capital in the way it was before 1979, and its current 'unproductiveness' in that sense is probably overrated. The definition of the informal sector is open to much questioning, and it, too, is certainly more 'productive', in almost whatever sense, than is often made out. Yet it is also clear that the early strategy of reconstruction maintained the focus on the cities. The Frente encouraged the urban poor, an important element of its social base, to make demands, and responded positively to them; in the country its early reforms maintained, even if they also transformed, the focus on Managua; and migration to the city continued. The strategy of survival has changed those priorities, and seems to be involving a real readjustment between urban and rural. Food production has certainly increased, and the new stage in the agrarian reform, by further improving conditions for the previously landless and the relatively poor in the countryside, may do something to restrain rural-urban migration. But the very same strategy implies less resources for the city. The spontaneous settlements of Managua are likely to remain a central element of the politics of transition in Nicaragua for some time to come.

References

BARRICADA. Lunes Socioeconómico is a special Monday section in the newspaper Barricada devoted to socio-economic analysis of Nicaraguan society. For the period May 1983 to May 1984 they have been collected together in book form Lunes Socio-Económico de Barricada, published by CIERA-BARRICADA, Managua, Nicaragua.

BAUMEISTER E., 1982, 'Notas para la discusión del problema agrario en Nicaragua', paper presented to the Third National Congress of Social Sciences, October, Managua, Nicaragua.

BAUMEISTER E., 1985, 'Estructuras productivas y Reforma Agraria en Nicaragua' in R.L. Harris and C. Vilas (eds.) La revolución en Nicaragua, Ediciones ERA, Mexico. Also published in English as Nicaragua: a revolution under seige, Zed Books, London, England.

BLACK G., 1981, Triumph of the people: the Sandinista revolution in Nicaragua, Zed Books, London, England.

CARMONA M., 1984, 'Aspectos para la caracterización de la realidad urbana: inventarización de las políticas de mejoramiento urbano dirigidas a los sectores de bajos recursos en Managua', mimeo, Technische Hogeschool, Delft, Netherlands.

CEPAL, 1981, Nicaragua: el impacto de la mutación política (Mexico: E/CEPAL/G.1147).

CEPAL, 1982, Características principales del proceso y de la política de industrialización de Centroamérica, 1960–1980. (Mexico: E/CEPAL/MEX 1982).

CIERA-MIDINRA, 1985, Sondeo en diez asentamientos, December, Managua, Nicaragua.

CIERA-UNRISD, 1984, 'Managua es Nicaragua', Managua, Nicaragua.

CONNOLLY P., 1985, 'The politics of the informal sector: a critique', in E. Mingione and N. Redclift (eds.), Beyond Employment, Allison and Busby, Oxford, pp.55–91.

CORRAGIO J.L., 1984, 'El sistema de acumulación en la transición: conceptos teóricos', paper presented to SSRC Workshop on Problems of transition in small peripheral societies, September.

DARKE R., with ALEXANDER D., DARKE J. and MANOGUE A., 1986, 'Housing in Nicaragua', Department of Urban Studies, University of Sheffield, England.

DEERE C.D. and MARCHETTI P., 1981, 'The worker-peasant alliance in the first year of the Nicaraguan Agrarian Reform', Latin American Perspectives, 29 (Spring), vol.III, no.2, pp.40-73.

DELFT, 1984, 'Plan Piloto', Barrio study of Managua, Technische Hogeschool, Delft, Netherlands.

ENVIO, 1986, 'Slow motion towards a survival economy', Envío, Instituto Histórico Centroamericano, vol.5, no.63, pp.13-38. September. Managua, Nicaragua.

FAUNE M.A., 1986, 'Agresión imperialista y campesinado en Nicaragua', Revista nicaragüense de ciencias sociales, ANICS (Asociación nicaraguense de científicos sociales), vol.1, no.1, pp.16-26.

HARRIS R.L., 1985, 'Transformación económica y desarrollo industrial de Nicaragua' in R.L. Harris and C. Vilas (eds.) La revolución en Nicaragua, Ediciones ERA, Mexico. Also published in English as 'The economic transformation and industrial development of Nicaragua' in R. Harris and C. Vilas (eds.) Nicaragua: a revolution under seige, Zed Books, London, England.

INEC, 1982, Encuesta de hogares, Managua, Nicaragua.

INIES, 1986, 'Los asentamientos espontáneos en Managua', INIES-Departamento de investigaciones urbanas, Revista nicaraguense de ciencias sociales, ANICS (Asociación nicaraguense de científicos sociales), vol.1, no.1, pp.78-86.

MARTIN J.L., 1981, 'Las tomas de terrenos urbanos en Managua', October, Managua, Nicaragua.

MINVAH, 1983, 'Antecedentes y Gestión', Managua, Nicaragua.

VILAS C., 1984, Perfiles de la revolución Sandinista, Casa de las Americas, Havana, Cuba.

WEEKS J., 1981, Análisis preliminar del desarrollo manufacturero 1960-1979, Managua, Nicaragua.

WHEELOCK J., 1976, Imperialismo y dictadura: crisis de una formación social, SIGLO XXI, Mexico City, Mexico.

WHEELOCK J., 1983, El gran desafío, Editorial Nueva Nicaragua, Managua, Nicaragua.

STOP PRESS*

As this book goes to press, news of Plans for 1987/8 have become available, and in a number of ways they are relevant to the discussion in preceding chapters.

At the most general level the Economic Plan 1987 stresses that the strategy remains one of survival. In this context the intention is announced of discontinuing investments which lack adequate funds. It is likely that this will include some of the large export-oriented projects. The Plan also announces measures which will attempt to extend taxation to cover the informal sector, which continues to grow, and to tighten up on evasion.

The housing ministry MINVAH has also published its plan and this contains a number of measures very relevant to the issues discussed in this book. Following the framework of the Economic Plan, in which regional priority is given to the war zones, the ministry's small construction budget is concentrated on activity in those areas. The sequence of priorities is housing needed for: defence, production, peasant cooperatives, agricultural, industrial and mining workers, and people displaced by the war. Because of the increased military activity by the Contra it is pointed out that some of the housebuilding programmes in the war zones may have to be postponed. Nonetheless it is clear that there is no money available for construction in Managua itself.

However, there are also other proposals. First, there is to be a programme to establish 'micro-regional systems'. These will link together dispersed settlements in rural areas. It is hoped that they will make production easier, and also defence, as well as cheapening the provision of basic infrastructure and services. Most importantly, it is hoped that they will help hold people in the countryside, reducing at least a little the flow of migration to the towns.

In Managua in the absence of any possibility of new building, the spontaneous settlements are to be reorganised, through plans drawn up at local level between MINVAH itself and the CDSs, in the context of the overall plan for the city drawn up by the local urban government (the Plan Contingente of the Alcaldía of Managua). Building materials will be made available to workers at subsidised prices, to enable better maintenance of houses, and the laws on tenancy and rents are to be revised.

The story continues

* Thanks to the Nicaraguan Solidarity Committee for help in obtaining this information.